I0521204

UNMUTED

&

UNBREAKABLE

The journey from Silenced, Struggling, & Surviving
to Soft, Strong, and Unapologetically HER

Latriecia Oliver (Triecia)

Unmuted & Unbreakable © 2025 Latriecia Oliver

ISBN:979-8-9935876-0-8

First Printing Edition: 2025

Scriptures are taken from the Holy Bible, New International Version® (NIV®) and King James Version® (KJV®), unless otherwise noted.

For questions, speaking engagements, or rights inquires, contact:

herpurposefulepursuit@gmail.com

Interested in personal development and coaching? Visit www.thebecomingherjourney.com to learn more about my programs and how we can work together.

To the woman who held back tears in the shower so her children would not hear her break. To the woman who stayed strong when life kept swinging, who sacrificed her own joy to make sure everyone else had what they needed. This book is for the woman who was never taught how to rest, how to feel, or how to receive love without earning it first. For the single mother with empty hands but a full heart, for the woman quietly piecing herself back together, for the soul who is tired yet still dares to dream, this is your soft place to land.

And to my daughters, Katrice and Khloé, I pray you grow up knowing your worth without ever having to fight so hard to prove it. I pray you choose peace over pain, joy over duty, and love without conditions. Your mother wrote this for every version of herself, versions she hopes you will never have to become.

Acknowledgments

To every tear that fell when no one was watching, thank you. To the silence that taught me how to hear God's whisper, thank you. To the woman who came before me and fought battles I will never fully know, this book is for you.

To my daughters, who make me brave even when I am tired. Watching you grow has pushed me to become more.

To the women who are still trying to figure it all out while holding everything together, thank you for existing. You are not alone. You are not too late. You are not forgotten.

To my tribe, my quiet encouragers, and every soul who spoke life into me during my lowest days, thank you for seeing me when I felt invisible.

To everyone who showed up in their own way, through wisdom, presence, or even their absence, thank you for your role in this becoming.

To my father. Your strength shaped my survival, and your sacrifices taught me what perseverance looks like. Your love was steady, even when the world was not. You held it down when life tried to break you, and I watched, learned, and grew stronger because of it.

To God, who isolated me, wrecked me, rebuilt me, and is now using me, I owe it all to You. Thank you for not giving up on me, even when I had given up on myself. I am nothing without You.

Foreword

By Triecia

I didn't write this book from the mountaintop. I wrote it with shaky hands, tear-stained hoodies, and heart-heavy nights when I wasn't sure if I would ever see peace again. There were moments I felt buried beneath responsibilities, motherhood, heartbreak, and the silent scream of dreams I couldn't afford to chase. But somewhere between survival mode and surrender, I heard God whisper, "Write."

This isn't just a book. It is a mirror, a balm, and a battle cry for the woman who is still in it. For the one trying to heal and build at the same time. For the one who looks strong on the outside but is quietly unraveling behind closed doors.

If you have ever felt like you were behind, too broken, or too far gone to create a life you love, this is for you.

I pray that every chapter feels like a hand reaching for yours in the dark. I pray you see your reflection in these pages and finally realize: you're not crazy. You're not weak. You're becoming.

You're not reading this by accident.

So breathe deep, sis.

Take your time.

Cry if you need to.

Highlight what speaks to you.

Dance around if it feels right.

Come back to it when you forget who you are.

I'll be here.

Every page.

Every step.

You're not doing this alone anymore.

With all my love,

Triecia

Introduction

This book isn't just words. It is a journey. And you, sis, are the reason it exists.

I don't know how you got here. Maybe you stumbled across this book by accident. Maybe a friend handed it to you at just the right time. Or maybe, deep down, you have known for a while that something had to change and this was the sign you were waiting for. Either way, welcome. You are not too late. You are not too broken. And no, you have not missed your moment.

This book is for the woman who is tired of surviving. The woman who shows up for everyone else while silently abandoning herself. The woman who has mastered "holding it together" but no longer remembers what rest feels like.

I wrote this for the woman who cries in the shower, pushes through the pain, and still dares to dream of more, even when life has tried to convince her that "more" is not meant for her.

For years, I lived in that space: overwhelmed, stretched thin, anxious, and constantly feeling as if I were falling short in every area of my life. I was the strong one. The dependable one. The woman who could make it happen no matter what. But what happens when the strong one starts to crack?

My healing did not begin in a therapist's office or at a retreat. It began in the garage. In silence. In surrender. With tears running down my face, hoodie sleeves soaked, asking God why He was letting me down.

And in that stillness, I heard Him say:

"You are not drowning. You are awakening. Your purpose is in your pain."

From that moment, everything began to shift. Not overnight, but one decision at a time.

This book is not about becoming perfect. It is about becoming whole. It is about shedding the masks, rewriting the narratives, and choosing peace over performance. It is about giving yourself permission to dream again and actually create a life that feels like yours.

Inside these pages, you'll find:

- Real-life reflections and raw truths.

- Practical tools and healing items.

- Affirmations and letters written straight from my soul to yours.

- And a story… one that might feel a little too familiar.

But more than anything, you will find yourself again. Buried beneath the expectations. Hidden under the pain. Waiting.

I will not promise this journey will be easy, but I can promise it will be worth it. And you will not be doing it alone. I am walking with you. Praying for you. Cheering like crazy every time you choose yourself.

You are not weak for needing this book.

You are brave for picking it up.

Let's begin.

With love,

Triecia

How to Use This Book

You don't have to rush. You just have to begin.

This book is designed to feel like a conversation - a sacred space where you can take off your mask, breathe deep, and come home to yourself.

Each chapter is layered with intention:

- **Real talk and raw reflection** to let you know you're not alone.

- **Practical tools and perspective shifts** to guide your healing in real time.

- **Affirmations and letters** to speak life back into the parts of you that feel forgotten.

- **Letters** written to the deepest parts of your soul to remind you of your strength, your softness, and your power.

I also created a workbook just for you which is available for purchase at www.serenity920.co.

There is no "right" way to read this book. But here's what I suggest:

- **Take your time**. One chapter a day. One letter a week. One affirmation on your mirror. Go at the pace your heart can handle.

- **Journal as you go**. Keep a notebook or your workbook nearby. Don't just read…respond. Let your thoughts, fears, and breakthroughs live on the page.

- **Revisit often**. Healing isn't linear. You'll grow, circle back, reread a letter and cry for a whole new reason. That's the beauty of becoming… there's always more waiting to unfold.

- **Highlight what hits**. Dog-ear the pages. Draw stars. Write in the margins. Make this book your own.

- **Don't skip the short story.** At the end of the book, you'll meet three women: Brielle, Jasmine, and Monique. Their lives are fictional, but their struggles are real. Their journey echoes yours, and together, their story brings this book full circle.

This is not just a book you read; it is a book you walk through. Let it hold your hand. Let it challenge you. Let it open you up.

Because somewhere inside these pages, I believe you will remember who you were before survival mode. You will reclaim who you are becoming. And you will realize that you have always been **Unmuted and Unbreakable.**

CONTENTS

Part 1:
The Becoming Begins

Chapter One

No One's Coming to Save You

"Faith without works is dead." James 2:26

Let me tell you something that shook me to my core the day I realized it: no one is coming to save me. Not the man you thought would step up. Not the family that said they would always have your back. Not the system. Not the job. Not the "perfect time" you keep waiting for. And definitely not the "right time" I was waiting on to finally choose myself. I had to stop waiting for help and start becoming my own rescue. I had to tell myself, "Girl, it is just you, but you are more than enough." And that is when my mission began.

In order to choose me, I had to stop waiting for someone to give me permission to live, to dream, to heal, or to grow. I was ready to step fully into my power, unapologetically. I began to make decisions that would make my life better. I began to put my own needs on the list—not just on the list, but at the very top of it. I began to set boundaries without guilt and to walk away from everything that drained me or severed me, even if it was familiar.

And last, but certainly not least, I began to invest in my peace, my purpose, and my potential. I discovered that choosing me was not selfish, it was sacred. It was the declaration that I am no longer willing to abandon myself for comfort, approval, or convenience of others. It is saying, "I matter. My dreams matter. My healing matters."

It is not just self-care, it is self-respect. It is not just empowerment, it is alignment.

The Breaking Point

There was a night I will never forget, when I sat on my bathroom floor in silence. My kids were asleep. The house was dark. And I was staring at my phone, waiting on a text that never came. I didn't want money. I didn't want flowers. I just wanted someone to say, "I see you. I got you." But it never came.

That was the moment I realized I was all I had. That was the moment I realized that if I didn't make a change, I would be stuck there forever. In that moment I realized my life was depending on me to make a difference. And it was time I started treating myself like I mattered. Even though I hadn't realized it before, I knew I mattered now.

I know what it's like to sit in silence and wonder how everything ended up on your shoulders. You didn't ask to be the strong one. You didn't ask to carry the weight of your kids, your bills, your broken heart, and your unspoken dreams. But here you are, carrying it anyway.

I want you to know that this chapter isn't written from a place of judgment. It's written from the battlefield. From a woman who cried while sitting on the bathroom floor and still had to get up and make breakfast. From a woman who begged God to send help, and when none came, realized that maybe the help was her all along.

Those nights when my mind was screaming and I was emotionally exhausted, spiritually drained, and financially barely holding it all together, I would sit at the edge of my bed, staring at ceilings and walls like they owed me answers. All I wanted was someone to see me. To show up for me. To take the pressure off for just one day. But nobody came.

And in that moment, I felt God's presence and knew I was the answer to my own prayer. I didn't understand it at first. But that moment changed everything.

You're not broken because you're doing it alone; you're becoming. The truth is, you're not behind; you're being built. Every moment you felt abandoned was also a moment God was redirecting you to your own strength. Waiting on someone to save you will keep you stuck. Saving yourself is when everything shifts.

The Mindset Shift: Rescue Ain't Coming But That's Power

We have been conditioned to wait. Wait for a partner to show up. Wait for the right time. Wait for vacation. Wait for things to get better on their own. But sis, what if I told you the very thing you are waiting on is already inside you? You don't need permission to start healing. In fact, sometimes things get so heavy and so hard that you realize you cannot wait for permission any longer. You don't need applause to pursue your purpose. You don't need a perfect plan to begin again.

Here's the truth: no one is coming to save you, and that is the most liberating news you will ever hear. Because now, you get to choose yourself. You get to build the life they said you couldn't have. You get to rise, even if no one claps for you.

The Wake-Up List: Rescue Me Reality Check

Let's pause and reflect. Grab your journal or notes app and answer these questions with full honesty. No filters. No fluff. Just truth. This is for you and your future self, no one else.

1. **What have I been waiting for someone else to do for me?** (Be honest. Are you waiting on someone to take responsibility? Love you right? Validate your worth?)

2. **What would it look like to stop waiting and start moving?** (Does it mean finally applying for that job? Starting that side hustle? Leaving that toxic situation?).

3. **Who do I need to forgive to move forward?** (Sometimes it's them. But most times… its you.)

The Start-Now Step: A Letter to Myself

I want you to write a letter. Title it: *"I Got You Now."* Write to the version of you that was tired. The version that waited for love. The version that hoped someone would come fix it all. Here's a start:

Dear Me,

I know you're exhausted. I know you've held it together when you had every reason to fall apart. But I want you to know something: I see you and I got you now. I won't abandon you anymore. From this day forward, we rise together.

Let the tears fall if they come. That's healing. That's power. That's your freedom beginning to speak.

The Reality of Single Motherhood: Not a Victim, But a Victor

To my fellow single mother, this chapter hits different for us. We don't have the luxury of waiting. We don't get "sick days" from parenting. There is no PTO. We can't afford to romanticize the idea that someone is going to walk in and fix what's broken. And yet, here we are, still building, still believing, still breaking cycles.

Don't let anyone make you feel like you're "less than" because you're doing it alone. You're not less than, you're legendary. You are the blueprint for what resilience looks like in real life.

Encouragement for the Climb

You may be climbing, crying, and cussing all in the same breath, but you're still climbing. You don't have to have it all figured out. You don't need to be perfect. You just need to keep moving. Keep believing. And if today all you do is read this and whisper, "I'm not giving up," then that's enough. Let that be your victory today.

HER Moment: Journal Prompt

What have I been waiting for someone else to fix, support, or see in me that I now know I have the power to address on my own? What does it mean to finally say, "I've got me," and actually believe it?

Closing words

This chapter wasn't meant to make you feel like you're alone. It's meant to remind you of the truth: you're not helpless, you're powerful. You don't have to be bitter. You don't have to be broken. And you definitely don't have to stay stuck. You can start again, even from the bottom.

In the next chapter, we'll dig into what it means to become *Her in the Dark*—how to grow when no one's clapping, no one's watching, and no one understands your journey. Until then, keep whispering this truth to yourself:

"I'm not waiting anymore. I'm walking in it."

A Letter to the Woman that's becoming HER... from the bottom

Hey you,

I hate to be the one to say this, but it has to be said... no one's coming to save you.

I had to learn that the hard way, sitting in my garage, completely undone. My hoodie sleeves were soaked from wiping tears that wouldn't stop falling, and my soul felt like it had been stepped on one too many times. I was waiting, hoping someone would show up. A friend, a parent, a partner, somebody to take some of the weight off. But no one came.

And that's when I realized... this wasn't punishment. It was an awakening. God didn't send someone to rescue me; He called me to rise. Not because I had it all together, but because He knew it was time for me to become the woman I kept waiting for.

Sis, I know how heavy it feels to carry everything alone. I know how easy it is to pray for a way out while quietly breaking on the inside. But here's the truth: you are not helpless. You are not hopeless. You are the answer to your own prayer.

This is your invitation to stop waiting to be chosen, saved, or rescued. You have been equipped, even in brokenness, to change your life. It will not happen overnight, and it will not always be pretty. But your power is real. And it starts the moment you stop waiting and start choosing you.

You did not flip this page by accident. You were led here.

Now… let's walk this thing out together.

With fire and love,

Triecia

Chapter Two

Becoming Her in the Dark

"It was in the dark that I finally found my light"

There's a silence that can swallow you whole. A stillness so heavy it feels like suffocation. That's where I found myself… not just tired, not just sad. I was buried beneath depression and anxiety so deep, I wasn't sure I'd ever rise again.

The world kept spinning. My kids still needed me. Work still expected me. Life didn't stop. But I was frozen inside. Crumbling silently in a world that expected me to keep functioning. And then one day, I ended up in the last place I thought I'd find God… my garage.

The Moment Everything Broke

I will never forget the night I sat in my garage. Not stood. Not paced. Sat. There was no plan for me to be out there. No dramatic storm of events. I had made it through the day like I always did, robotically. Fed the kids. Wiped counters. Smiled when I wanted to scream. But inside, I was unraveling in slow motion. I needed space. A place to fall apart without an audience. So I walked out into the garage, pulled a worn-out chair into the center of the floor, and quietly shut the door behind me.

I didn't bring my phone. I didn't even turn on the light. I just sat there in the dark, in the cold, in the silence. And then I broke. I collapsed into that chair like it was the only thing keeping me from crumbling to the ground. At first, it was a single tear. Then another. And before I knew it, I was sobbing, loud, breathless, gut-wrenching cries that echoed off the garage walls.

I wasn't crying like a woman having a bad day. I was crying like a woman whose soul had been carrying far too much for far too long. The kind of cry where your body goes limp and your mind just whispers, "I'm done." I buried my face in the sleeves of my hoodie, trying to muffle the sound, but it didn't matter. The pain was louder than my pride. I cried so hard, so long, that by the end of it my hoodie sleeves were soaked. Not damp but wet from wiping away wave after wave of tears. That hoodie caught the pieces of me I didn't know I needed to release — years of exhaustion, silent battles, unspoken grief, shattered dreams, and the deepest ache of all, feeling like I had been forgotten.

Through the sobs I whispered, "God, why? Why does this hurt so bad? Why do I feel so alone? Why me?" I didn't need theology. I didn't need a motivational quote. I needed to know that heaven hadn't turned its back on me. And in the stillness, as I sat in that chair with tear-soaked sleeves and a shattered heart, I didn't hear God audibly, but I felt Him. Right there in the cold, cement-floored garage, He met me. Not to shame me. Not to scold me. But to sit with me. And in the deepest part of my spirit, I heard these words like a whisper carried on the wind:

"I isolated you… so I could rebuild you. I needed your attention. And now that I have it… let's begin."

When God Pulls You Away to Pull You Together

At the time, I thought I was being abandoned, left to carry everything alone. But now I know I was being positioned. God had to quiet the noise. He had to remove the people I was leaning on too heavily. He had to strip away the things I thought I needed so I could discover who I truly was without them. In the dark, He started His work. And the first thing He did was help me see… me.

The sacredness of Darkness

Darkness doesn't always mean disaster. Sometimes, darkness is the delivery room for destiny. God does His deepest work in hidden places. And when you're isolated, when no one's watching, when there's no applause, that's where He rebuilds you from the inside out. In the darkness, I learned that:

- Healing doesn't always feel like healing. Sometimes it feels like being emptied first.

- Peace isn't always loud. Sometimes it comes in complete stillness.

- Becoming her - the woman I always wanted to be, required losing the version of me that was trying to survive instead of thrive.

The Rebuild: My healing Process

Here's what I began to do - slowly, imperfectly, but consistently:

1. I got honest with God. I stopped praying like I had it together. I started crying out like a daughter in need of her Father. And I felt Him closer that I ever had before.

2. I created space to feel. That garage became my sacred space. My chair, my tears, my truth. No filters. No masks. Just me and God.

3. I wrote it out. Every emotion. Every question. Every ounce of pain. I started journaling and discovering that healing happens when the truth hits paper.

4. I gave myself permission to pause. I stopped performing for people who didn't see my pain. I started setting boundaries. I gave myself room to breathe.

HER Moment: Journal Prompt

What was my "garage" moment, the place where I broke down and finally invited God in? What did He reveal to me in the silence? What parts of me have grown stronger in the dark?

Garage Chair Reflection Exercise

Find a quiet space, alone. Sit in stillness. Close your eyes and go back to your own "garage moment." Then, answer the following:

1. What emotions came up that I've been avoiding?

2. What lie about myself or my life did I release in that moment?

3. What did God begin to show me about who I really am?

"She was never lost. Just hidden. Planted deep in the dark. Until the day she realized... she was meant to bloom in silence."

Closing Words

The dark is not pretty. It's heavy, it's lonely, and it will make you question if God even remembers your name. It will have you up at 3 a.m. looking at the ceiling, wondering why you have to be the strong one all the time. It's that place where your chest feels like it's caving in, and no matter how loud you scream inside, the world keeps moving like you don't even exist.

But the dark? It's also where you start to see yourself for real. Not the version you present to everybody else, but the raw, messy, don't-have-it-all-together version. And you know what? That version is the one who's becoming. That version is the one God is shaping. You might feel buried, but the truth is... you're planted. And one day, what you grew through is going to be the very thing that saves another woman who's sitting in her own dark.

You don't have to like the dark, but don't you dare forget it made you.

Letter to the Becoming you

Let me talk to you plain: I know what it feels like when the darkness will not let up. When you drag yourself out of bed, put on the smile, go to work, cook dinner, check homework, do all the things, and still crawl under the covers at night feeling empty. I know what it is like to cry into a pillow so nobody hears you. I know what it is like to keep it together for your kids while you are breaking apart in silence. I know what it is like to beg God, "When is it my turn to breathe?"

I am not here to sell you a fairy tale. The dark does not disappear overnight. But you need to know this: you are not weak for being here. You are not crazy for feeling like you cannot take another hit. You are not broken beyond repair. You are in process. You are in becoming.

The world tries to make you believe that being "her" only happens in the light, when the bills are paid, when the house is clean, when your edges are laid, when your smile looks Instagram perfect. But no. Becoming happens here, in the ugly, in the lonely, in the nights that feel like they will swallow you whole.

So do not give up. Do not give in. If you have to crawl through the dark, crawl. If you have to cry through it, cry. If you have to scream in your car, scream. Just do not stop moving. Because even in the dark, you are becoming. And one day, when the light hits you, you will look back and realize you were not just surviving, you were being built.

Hold on. The light is closer than you think.

You're biggest fan

Triecia

Chapter Three

Healing While Holding It All Together

"Come to me, all you who are weary and burdened, and I will give you rest." Matthew 11:28

She's the one who shows up, even when her heart is breaking. Even when she's exhausted, overlooked, or unraveling on the inside, she still gets up. She still pours. She still holds it together.

This chapter is for *her.*

The Pain of the Functioning Wounded

You ever feel like you're bleeding emotionally but still expected to be everything for everybody?

Like your soul is quietly unraveling in the background while your body is still clocking in, cooking dinner, folding laundry, and trying to smile for the kids?

It's one of the heaviest kinds of pain—healing from wounds you didn't ask for while life keeps demanding more of you.

The world doesn't pause for your healing. But you must.

Because if you don't, something breaks. And this time, it might be you.

My Healing Wasn't Loud. It Was Lit.

My healing didn't come from some big moment. It came in the in-between late nights when the house was finally quiet, in the mornings where I sat in stillness before the world woke up. There was one thing that kept me grounded.

I lit candles and I wrote.

That's how it began. I didn't always have words. Sometimes I just wrote what hurt. Other times, I wrote what I hoped for. And every time I lit a candle, I imagined it burning away the chaos and lighting up the parts of me that felt dim.

Eventually, those quiet stillness sessions turned into healing practices, and those practices became the foundation of what would one day grow into a business.

But back then?

It wasn't about profit.

It was about peace.

To the Woman Holding it All Together

I see you. You're healing from heartbreak, trauma, and disappointment. You're grieving the support you never had, the partner who never showed up, the version of your life you imagined by now. And on top of that… you're still working, parenting, cleaning, cooking, surviving.

You may not have a luxury retreat. You may not get a break. But that doesn't mean you can't heal. You don't need perfect conditions. You just need intention.

Practical Ways to Heal in the Middle of the Chaos

Let's make this real. Here's how you start healing while still showing up for everything and everyone:

1. Set Micro-Moments for Yourself (2-5 minutes): Healing doesn't always need hours. Start with 5 minutes before bed, or 3 minutes in the car after drop-off. Use that time to breathe, journal, cry, pray - or do nothing. The pause is the point.

2. Journal Without Pressure: Don't worry about grammar. Write what's real. Try simple prompts like:

    *   "Right now, I feel…"

    *   "Today drained me because…"

    *   "I wish someone would just…"

Even 5 sentences can set you free.

3. Light Something That Grounds You. A candle. Incense. Oil. The goal isn't just the scent… it's the symbol. Let that flame remind you: I'm allowed to reset. I'm allowed to rest. I'm allowed to release.

4. Saying No Without Explaining boundaries is healing in motion. You don't owe anyone access to your energy when you're in recovery. "No" is a full sentence. Say it and mean it. Let it free you.

5. Ask For Help… Even If It Feels Awkward. If you're drowning in silence, speak. Whether it'a friend, a therapist, or a trusted coach… get support. You don't have to prove your strength by suffering in silence.

6. Don't Rush the Process: Healing is messy. Some days you'll feel strong. Other days, you'll want to quit everything and everyone. Both are normal. Keep showing up anyway.

HER Moment: Jornal Prompt

What part of me am I pretending is "fine" but still needs healing? What would it look like to create space for that healing in small, practical ways? What do I need to give myself permission to release today?

Closing Words

You don't have to disappear to deserve healing. You don't have to escape your life to begin restoring it. You just have to stop ignoring your own heart.

That's what I did, one night at a time. One tear-soaked journal page at a time. One candle flame at a time.

And maybe today... you start with this chapter. And a whisper to yourself that says:

"I'm worthy of healing... even while I'm holding everything else together."

Letter to the woman that's healing while holding it all together

I don't even know how you're still standing, but you are. You're healing with a full plate, an aching heart, and barely any sleep. You're showing up for people who don't even notice you breaking. You're making things work with scraps. You're holding back tears at work. You're pushing through exhaustion like it's normal, like your burnout doesn't even deserve rest.

But I see you and so does God. Don't let the silence fool you. Heaven has been watching you fight. I know what it feels like to be mid-breakdown but still cooking dinner. To cry in the car before walking in the house like everything is fine. To scroll your phone at night looking for some sign that somebody gets it, that you're not the only one growing quietly.

I remember dragging myself to the bathroom, closing the door, and just sitting there in the dark. Not even crying sometimes. Just there. Numb. Beaten. Spent. Trying to figure out how to fix everything when I didn't even have the strength to fix me.

Healing while holding it all together is one of the hardest things a woman will ever do. Because it means you don't get to fall apart, not really. You have to break in pieces, quietly, and still show up whole for everybody else.

But please listen to me. You are allowed to rest. You are allowed to feel. You are allowed to say, "I can't do it all," and still be powerful. You are allowed to light a candle, sit in silence, and let the tears fall without shame. You don't have to earn peace; it's your birthright.

You've carried more than your fair share. You've smiled through grief and pushed through drama. And even though the world never gave you time to slow down, I'm giving it to you now.

Stop for a second, close your eyes, and breathe, sis. This letter is proof that somebody out here understands the storm you're standing in. And I need you to know: your healing matters. Even if it's slow. Even if it's messy. Even if no one claps for it.

I'm walking it with you, every step of the way. Keep going even if you have to do it with shaky hands and tear-stained cheeks. You're not just surviving, you're becoming.

And the woman you're becoming?

She's worth everything.

With my whole heart,

Triecia

Chapter Four

Peace Over Performance

"You are allowed to be a masterpiece and a work in progress at the same time." - Sophia Bush

You've been applauded for being strong. Celebrated for showing up. Admired for how much you can carry. But let me ask you something real: Are you performing strength or living in peace? Because somewhere along the way, "strong" became our identity. But what we call strength is sometimes just survival in disguise.

The Performance You Didn't Realize You Were Giving

There's a performance that no one sees. It's in the way you respond to "How are you?" with a forced "I'm good." It's in the way you keep pushing through headaches, heartbreaks, and hard days just to keep everything afloat. It's exhausting to live like that. To feel like your value is attached to how much you do. To show up to a job that drains you, cook for kids who don't say thank you, and go to bed praying for the strength to repeat it

24

tomorrow. All while no one claps for your effort, but you keep performing anyway.

My Peace Wasn't Loud. It Was a Quiet Fight

Let me be honest, I didn't wake up one day and decide I wanted peace. I just got tired. Tired of explaining myself. Tired of pretending I wasn't hurt. Tired of showing up strong when I was falling apart. I remember one afternoon, I was sitting in my car, the kids in the back seat arguing, my phone buzzing with notifications from work, family, and friends who needed something, and I just went still. I wasn't angry. I wasn't sad. I was done.

That's the moment I realized I had been performing, not for applause but for survival. That's when I started reaching for peace. Not the peace you post about on social media. Not the "bubble bath and wine" peace. But the kind that says:

"I will no longer betray myself to keep others comfortable"

What Peace Really Means (Not Just Feels Like)

Peace isn't always pretty. It's not always soft music, candlelight, and a cup of tea. Sometimes peace is messy. It's choosing to say no to people you love. It's disappointing others to honor your own needs. It's removing yourself from conversations that feel like combat. It's turning off your phone and letting the world exist without your constant availability.

Peace is not passive. It's a discipline. It's a decision. And it's a declaration:

"I will protect my peace like I protect my children... Fiercely and without apology"

To the Woman Who's Still Proving Herself

Sis, what are you trying to prove, and to who? That you're strong? You already are. That you can handle it all? You've been doing that. That you're not lazy, emotional, too much, or not enough? Here's the truth: You don't have to earn rest. You don't have to deserve peace. You just have to stop giving your energy to people, places, and pressures that do not pour back into you.

You're Not Lazy- You're Tired of the Show

When peace becomes the goal, performance loses its grip. You start saying no without guilt. You stop explaining your boundaries. You quit chasing validation. You stop overthinking yourself just to feel like you're "enough."

Let me say this plainly: you're not lazy. You're tired of the show. And your peace is proof that you finally value your life more than you value being liked.

Performance Shows Up in Disguises

Lets go deeper. Performance isn't just "doing the most." It hides in everyday habits:

- Overbooking your calendar so you feel "productive"

- Always being available so people don't think you're selfish

- Doing everything alone because asking for help makes you feel weak

- Cleaning before guest come over so they think you're put together

- Posting on social media so it looks like your thriving

    Pause.

Which of these are you doing? And why? Now ask yourself: What would change if I didn't feel the need to prove anything to anyone?

Practical Peace Practices (Real Talk, Real Life)

Let's talk about how to actually build a lifestyle rooted in peace, not just moments of it.

1. Start Your Day *With* You, Not the World: Before checking your phone, tune in to your own voice. Say a prayer. Sit in Silence. Stretch. Even five minutes. It sets the tone: *"I belong to me first today."*

2. Create Your "No for Now" List: Write down the things that are not aligned with you peace right now- even if you used to say yes. Examples:

- Volunteering for things out of guilt

- Conversations that go nowhere but drain your energy

- Last-minute obligations that throw off your rhythm

Your sanity is not up for negotiation.

3. Simplify Where You're Over-performing: Are you overdoing meals? Laundry? House expectations? Can you order out? Use paper plates? Take a night off from being supermom? Give yourself permission to simplify.

4. Create an End-of-Day Wind-Down: This is where "Unwind & Align" comes in. Light your candle. Write three things:

- What drained you

- What fed you

- What you're releasing before bed

This practice changed my life.

5. Choose Rest On Purpose: Rest isn't what you do when you collapse. Rest is what you choose when you value your body, your mind, and you presence.

Schedule it. Honor it. Let people adjust.

HER Moment: Journal Prompt

Where in my life am I over-performing or over-explaining myself? What lie am I believing that's keeping me stuck instead of peaceful? What would my life look like if I truly chose peace without guilt?

Your Peace Plan: Rewritten Truths to Live By

Here's you new belief system. Print it. Recite it. Live it.

- I do not have to earn rest.

- Saying "no" protects my peace and honors my soul.

- Being unavailable is sometimes the most powerful boundary I can set.

- God is not impressed by burnout. He's drawn to surrender.

- My worth is not tied to my productivity.

Peace is my *birthright,* not a luxury.

Closing Words

Let this be the chapter that sets you free. Free from chasing, performing, proving, explaining, and over-functioning. Free from the invisible weight of being "the strong one." You don't have to keep performing to matter. You don't have to keep pushing to be powerful.

Your peace is your power. So when the next moment comes and you have to choose between being impressive or being in alignment, between being busy or being whole, between making others comfortable or honoring your own needs... choose peace. Every. Single. Time.

"She wasn't angry. She was at peace. And that silence was louder that any performance she'd ever given."

Letter to the woman who's tired of performing

How long have you been wearing that mask? How long have you been clapping for others with an empty cup? Showing up strong because "rest" is not in your vocabulary? Smiling just enough to keep people from asking questions, but dying inside from the weight of pretending?

Yeah, I've been there.

I used to think if I did enough, achieved enough, proved enough... maybe then I'd feel worthy. Maybe then the anxiety would back off. Maybe then I'd sleep through the night.

But peace doesn't come when you earn it. Peace comes when you choose it.

There's a whole version of you that exists beyond the hustle. Beyond the to-do list. Beyond performance. She's the one who breathes deeper. Who laughs from her belly. Who journals without guilt. Who lights a candle not to mask the chaos, but to honor her healing.

And let me tell you something you've probably never been told: you don't have to earn softness, nor do you have to deserve rest. You don't need another gold star to finally be "enough." You already are.

Peace isn't a reward for doing it all. It's your right for surviving it all. So please, sis, lay it down. The cape. The checklist. The heavy expectations. None of that determines your value.

Peace feels like finally giving yourself permission to just be. No striving. No proving. No pretending. Just you, in all your raw, unfiltered glory.

So today, let this be your reminder: you are not a machine. You are not a performance. You are not what you produce. You are a woman who deserves peace in her bones and joy in her spirit — not just when the work is done, but right now.

Choose it. Protect it. Reclaim it.

The world can wait. Your peace can't.

With so much love,

Triecia

Chapter Five

Soft Life, Hard Choices

"She is clothed with strength and dignity; she can laugh at the days to come." Proverbs 31:25

The life you want is on the other side of the decisions you're afraid to make.

What is the Soft Life, Really?

Let's clear this up first. The soft life is not just champagne and silk robes. It's not just candles, brunch aesthetics, or travel reels. The soft life is peace. It's ease. It's living without constantly bleeding yourself dry for other people. It's waking up without anxiety being your alarm clock. It's no longer choosing survival when thriving is your birthright. It's a life built on alignment, not hustle. But here's what nobody tells you: softness is a choice, and often, it's the hardest choice you'll find.

Why the Soft Life Feels So Hard to Choose

When you've spent your whole life fighting, protecting, proving, and surviving, softness can feel dangerous. Like weakness. Like laziness. Like you're letting something go before it's "safe" to relax.

Here's the truth: softness isn't weakness. It's wisdom. It says, "I don't have to break myself to be valuable." It says, "I've earned a life where I don't constantly have to suffer to prove I'm strong."

But to live that life, you've got to make some hard decisions.

The Hard Choices Behind the Soft Life

1. Walking Away From What's Comfortable But Draining: That job, that friendship, that relationship- if it constantly empties you, it's not meant for your soft life.

2. Saying No Without Explaining Yourself: Soft living requires boundaries. And boundaries will offend people who were benefiting from your lack of them.

3. Choosing Rest When the World Worships Grind: Softness means choosing a nap over another task. It means turning off your phone- even when you feel guilty. It means understanding that rest is *productive* too.

4. Releasing Your Attachment to Struggle: Some of us are trauma-bonded to the hustle. If it isn't hard, we question if its real. Let that mindset go. You are allowed to receive with ease.

5. Detaching From "Strong Woman" Culture: You don't have to do it all. You don't have to know it all. You don't have to carry it all.

Sis, I Know You've Had to Be Hard

Hard to survive. Hard to parent alone. Hard to keep your walls up. Hard to not fall apart when no one's coming to save you. But you're safe to soften now. Not because life is perfect. Not because help magically showed up. But because you are choosing peace over pain.

And softness isn't for the weak. Softness is for the woman who's been through hell and is still choosing joy over jadedness.

How to Begin Living the Soft Life (Right Now)

You don't have to move to Bali or become a minimalist overnight. Here's how to begin:

1. Audit Your Energy: Who drains you? What depletes you? Where do you feel tense or resentful? Make a list. Be honest. Now start removing or reducing what doesn't serve peace.

2. Build Peace Into Your Schedule: Create sacred windows of softness- daily. Morning stretch and silence. A slow lunch without your phone. A 5 minute candle lite unwind moment before bed. You don't need a spa, you need daily softness.

3. Speak Softness Over Yourself

   - "I don't have to over perform today"

   - "I choose grace over guilt"

   - "My rest is sacred, not selfish"

4. Create Soft Goals, Not just Hustle Goals

   - Soft goal: I want to feel calm when I wake up.

   - Soft goal: I want to have enough income that allows me to rest when I need to.

   - Soft goal: I want relationships that feel easy, not earned

5. Build Income That Honors Your Soft Life

Whether its starting a business, launching a product, or monetizing your gifts, you don't need to break yourself to build wealth. Start creating income streams that don't require burnout. Remember, freedom funds softness.

HER Moment: Journal Prompt

What's one "hard" thing I know I need to walk away from to live softer? Where have you been choosing hustle over alignment? What would it look like if I gave myself permission to soften?

Closing Words

The soft life is not a trend. It's a radical, holy decision to live in wholeness, not hustle. To let your heart breathe again. To wake up and not feel dread. To live like peace isn't something you wait for, it's something you build.

So yes, the soft life comes with hard choices. But every time you choose softness over suffering, alignment over applause, and rest over rush, you're rewriting your story. And you're giving other women permission to do the same.

"She softened, not because life got easier, but because she got stronger about what she would no longer accept."

A Letter to the Woman Craving a Softer Life

I know you're tired of surviving. Tired of carrying it all. Tired of wondering if the "soft life" is just a fantasy for other women. The ones without the responsibilities. The ones with help. The ones who don't have to make magic out of crumbs.

But let me tell you something real: the soft life isn't just about spa days and pretty things. It's about peace and rest that don't come with guilt. It's about joy that doesn't come with a price tag. It's about choosing you… even when it feels selfish, even when it costs something.

And it will cost something. It will cost people-pleasing. It will cost overworking. It will cost late scrolling that soothes you but doesn't fill you. It will cost some relationships. It might even cost the comfort of who you used to be.

But what do you gain? You gain your time. You gain your mind. You gain space to feel, to grow, to bloom.

I remember sitting with my head in my hands wondering, "How do I even get there? How do I go from chaotic days and exhausted nights to something soft?"

The truth? I had to make some hard choices. I had to sacrifice comfort now for peace later. I had to say no when it broke my heart. I had to trust that rest was productive. I had to believe I deserved better even when my life didn't reflect it yet. And sis, you can too.

You are not too late. You are not too broken. You are not too far gone. The soft life is built one choice at a time. It's built in the moments you protect your peace, guard your time, and stop apologizing. You're not crazy for wanting ease. You're not lazy for craving rest. You're not ungrateful for dreaming bigger than what's in front of you.

You're just ready. And I see you. And I'm proud of you. So take the first step, even if it's small. Say the hard no. Choose the long game. Show up for yourself even when nobody claps.

Because every soft life starts with one hard choice: believing you're worth it.

With love and softness,

Triecia

Chapter Six

Letting Go of the Woman You Were Told to Be

"Forget the former things; do not dwell on the past. See, I am doing a new thing…" - Isaiah 43:18-19

You don't have to become who they expected. You are allowed to become who you were created to be.

There's a version of you that was built in survival. A version that made herself small to keep the peace. A version that took care of everyone else and learned to celebrate the crumbs. A version that was shaped by what they told you a woman should be: quiet, selfless, strong, grateful no matter what. But sis, that version was never the full story.

The Woman You Were Told to Be

Maybe she was the woman who stayed quiet, even when her soul was screaming. Maybe she was the strong one, even when she wanted to fall apart. Maybe she was the responsible one, always sacrificing, always showing up, even when no one showed up for her. Maybe she was the one who never chased her dreams because she was too busy helping everyone else chase theirs.

Or maybe she was taught to survive, not shine. To settle, not soar. They praised her. They leaned on her. But she was never seen.

Where Did That Version of You Come From?

She didn't come out of nowhere. She came from:

- Family Expectations: "Don't be too loud." "Be strong like your mama."

- Cultural Conditioning: "Black women don't have time to fall apart."

- Religious guilt: "Good women submit, sacrifice, and don't question."

- Generational trauma: "We survived, why can't you?"

- Childhood pressure: "Be mature." "Be helpful." "Be quiet." "Be good."

She was shaped by systems that never considered your soul. And it's not your fault you became her. But now, it's your responsibility to release her.

The Grief of Letting Go

Here's the part most people won't tell you: Letting go of the woman you were told to be will feel like grief. Because you've built a life around her. You've gotten applause of her. You've stayed in relationships, jobs, friendships, just to keep her image intact. So when you start peeling her off, piece by piece, you may feel:

- Guilty

- Ungrateful

- Confused

- Lonely

- Even lost

But sis, that's not failure. That's freedom stretching.

Who You Really Are... Is Underneath the Mask

She's the woman who speaks up even if her voice shakes, chooses joy even when it's inconvenient, builds boundaries and keeps them, honors her body, her dreams, and her heart, and asks for what she needs without apology.

She's not new. She's remembering. She's returning. You are not becoming someone different. You are becoming who you've always been.

Letting Go Looks Like

- Saying, "That's not me anymore" even if they don't understand.

- Making space for silence so you can hear your own voice again.

- Doing what feels right, not what looks right.

- Releasing guilt over choosing yourself.

- Redefining what "success" and "strength" really mean to you.

Letting go isn't just about leaving behind the past, it's about creating new patterns of the future.

Practice Ways to Release Her

Lets make it real. Here's how you be begin to let go of the woman you were told to be:

1. Write a Goodbye Letter to Her: Start with, *"You helped me survive, but I don't need you to lead anymore."* Thank her. Then release her. Let the tears come if they need to.

2. Make a "Not Me Anymore" List. Write out the things you no longer subscribe to:

   - "I don't say yes out of guilt anymore."

- "I don't shrink to make others comfortable."

- "I don't pretend I'm okay when I'm not."

3. Say yes to the New You, Out Loud. Affirm her daily.

    - "I am allowed to change my mind."

    - "I choose joy over performance."

    - "I no longer hustle for love or approval."

4. Take One Bold Step Toward the Woman you Want to Be: Apply for the job. Start the business. Take the solo trip. Book the therapy session. Post the video. Say the hard thing.

Every bold step chips away at the mask - and reveals her.

HER Moment: Journal Prompt

Who is the version of me I was "taught" to be? And what did it cost me? What beliefs, habits, or roles am I ready to let go of? Who is the woman underneath it all - an what does she want?

Closing Words

There's nothing wrong with you. There's just a version of you that was created to protect you. And now that you're healing, you don't need her anymore.

Letting go doesn't mean dishonoring your past. It means finally giving yourself permission to grow beyond it.

You are not selfish. You are not rebellious. You are becoming.

To the Woman Tired of Wearing a Mask

Who told you that you had to shrink to be accepted? That you had to smile through pain to be strong? That your softness was a weakness? That being "a good woman" meant staying quiet, staying small, and staying put?

Whoever it was, it's time to let her go. That version of you built out of their fears and expectations? You've been performing. Showing up for roles you never auditioned for. Playing nice to stay liked. Dimming your light because it made others squint. But deep down, you've always known. There's a real you buried under all that pretending. And she's fighting to come out.

Letting go of the woman you were told to be isn't rebellion. It's resurrection. You are not just somebody's mama. Not just somebody's daughter. Not just a worker, a fixer, a good girl, a strong Black woman, or whatever title they handed you.

You are becoming. And that means shedding. You will lose some people. You'll confuse a few. You might even scare yourself at first. But the freedom on the other side? Whew.

Sis, you are allowed to change your mind. To rewrite your story. To create a life that feels like yours. Even if nobody understands it but you. You owe yourself the truth. You owe yourself the joy. You owe yourself the peace of waking up every day as the woman you were always meant to be.

So here's your permission slip. Signed in courage. Delivered in love. Rip off the costume. Burn the script. And walk — no, strut — into the woman you are becoming. She's waiting for you. And baby, she's bad.

With Freedom and Fire,

Triecia

Chapter Seven

Time & Financial Freedom Isn't a Dream- It's a Discipline

"Discipline is choosing between what you want now and what you want most." - Abraham Lincoln

You don't just stumble into freedom. You build it. Brick by brick. Budget by budget. Boundary by boundary. And let's be real, it's not always glamorous. It doesn't always feel "soft." But it is necessary.

Time freedom. Financial peace. Waking up with options, not obligations. That's not a fantasy. That's the reward for the woman who decided, *"I'm done just surviving."*

The Truth About Freedom

A lot of people want freedom, but they don't want the structure it requires. But here's the paradox: discipline creates freedom. You don't earn peace through chaos. You don't buy time by wasting it. We've romanticized the idea of success, but we haven't respected the process of getting there.

And sis, the process requires focus.

What Time & Financial Freedom Really Looks Like

Let's break it down. Freedom isn't just about quitting your job or making six figures. Its about choices. Alignment. Control over your own life.

Time Freedom look like:

- Having a slow morning without panic or pressure

- Saying "yes" because you want to, not because you need to

- Attending your child's game without begging your boss

- Having time to rest without guilt

Financial freedom looks like:

- Paying bills on time without juggling miracles

- Creating income that doesn't exploit your energy

- Choosing what you *want* to do, not what you *have* to do

- Investing in your peace, not just your survival

But Let's Be Honest: It Requires a Shift

You don't reach this life by wishing. You get there by choosing…daily.

Choosing to:

- Wake up when you'd rather sleep

- Budget when you'd rather swipe

- Say no when you'd rather people-please

- Show up online when you feel insecure

- Build your business, post your content, make your offer- scared but consistent

It's not about being perfect. It's about being *disciplined enough to keep going when its not cute.*

The Real Struggles of Getting There (Especially as a MOM)

Let's Talk Real-Life:

- You're juggling a job, a household, and probably doing it all solo.

- You're tired.

- Your time feels stretched.

- Your money feels tight.

- Your dreams feel far away.

But here's the key: Every day you show up with intention is a deposit into your freedom account. Even if it's 30 minutes a day. Even if it's $10 a week into savings. Even if it's just saying no to something that drains you. Small steps. Big results.

Discipline Isn't Punishment- It's a Promise

It's not about forcing yourself, it's about reminding yourself: "I'm building the life I prayed for"

That vision you have? It's going to require:

- A better morning routine

- Boundaries with your time

- A financial strategy

- Focus on your income-producing work

- Saying "not right now" to things that look good but don't align

Freedom doesn't mean *easy*. It means *intentional*.

Your Freedom Plan: Practical Steps to Start Now

1. Time Audit

Where is your time going? What's draining you that isn't producing results or peace? Identify one time-waster and replace it with something aligned.

2. Create Non-Negotiable Time Blocks:

Give your dream a spot on the calendar. Even if it's 30 minutes a day. If it's not scheduled, it won't grow.

3. Budget for Peace:

Where is your money going? Start telling every dollar where to go: saving, investing, creating freedom-not just covering struggle.

4. Build the Income Streams

You already have a gift. A message. A product. Whether it's candles, coaching, content, or creativity-start building it now. Small steps matter: one product, one post, one payment.

5. Create "Freedom Routines"

Start treating your business, finances, and future with intention.

- Sunday planning session

- Weekly financial check-in

- Daily priority list

- Monthly vision reset

The woman with a vision always moves differently.

HER Moment Journal Prompt

What habits or distractions are robbing me of my freedom? What would my life look like if I honored my time and money more intentionally? What small step can I take this week toward the future I want?

Closing Words

This isn't about grinding. This is about growing.

Discipline isn't here to punish you. It's here to protect you, to position you, to build a bridge between where you are and where you know you're called to be. Every sacrifice you make for your freedom is a seed. And when it blooms, you'll thank the version of you who refused to quit.

"She built the life they said she couldn't have because she showed up when no one was watching."

A Letter to the Woman Tired of Counting Pennies and Minutes

You weren't born just to pay bills and die. You know that, right? But I also know what it feels like to be stuck in a loop. Clocking in at a job that drains your soul. Swiping your card and praying it doesn't decline. Waking up tired, going to sleep worried, and calling it "normal life."

Let's be real... we were taught survival, not freedom. We watched our parents stretch meals and mend pain in silence. We saw tiredness treated like a badge of honor. We were told to be grateful for crumbs, when we were born to feast.

Listen to me closely and carefully... freedom is not a fantasy. It's a decision. A discipline. A daily choice. It starts with believing that your time is valuable. That your peace is non-negotiable. That your dreams are not some wild delusions... they're divine direction.

It means skipping brunch sometimes to buy inventory. It means trading Netflix for knowledge. It means sacrificing comfort now so your future self can rest.

Time and financial freedom don't fall out of the sky. They come from getting dead serious about your life. They come from budgeting when your check is already stretched. From waking up an hour earlier to build that dream before the kids wake up. From making ten dollars work like a hundred, because your vision said so.

You don't need a degree in finance. You need discipline. You need belief. You need to stop saying "one day" and start saying "day one." You've got everything you need already inside you. God didn't plant the vision in you for nothing. He just needs your yes, your work, and your faith that doesn't fold.

You deserve to own your time. To breathe without asking permission. To leave generational scars behind and build generational wealth.

So start now… messy, scared, and unsure. But start.

Your freedom isn't just possible. It's coming for you… if you've got the guts to go get it. Let's build this life, brick by brick.

In grind and grace,

Triecia

Chapter Eight

Becoming Her While Still in Progress

"Being confident of this, that He who began a good work in you will carry it on to completion." -Philippines 1:6

You want to know something that not enough people talk about? How hard it is to hold on to a vision when your life still looks messy. You want to become her... the woman who's healed, aligned, thriving, soft, powerful... but today you're juggling past-due bills, work stress, mom guilt, relationship tension, and maybe even your own mental health struggles.

You don't feel like her. You feel like survival.

But let me tell you something I had to learn in my own journey: becoming is not clean. It's messy. It's shaky. It's faith in motion.

Your Freedom Plan: Practical Steps to Start Now

We look at woman we admire and think, "Wow, she's so put together." But we don't see her behind closed doors. We don't see:

- The tears she cried when the money didn't stretch

- The mom guilt she wrestled with when she chose her dream over another activity

- The late nights she worked while feeling like she should be resting

- The small, silent win she celebrated alone because nobody clapped for her yet

Sis, hear me: You are not failing because it's messy. You are becoming.

My Own Story: Wins + Wounds

I remember when I first started chasing my dream of building my business. I had so little time, so little money, so little energy. I would beat myself up when I missed a moment with my kids because I was working. I felt guilty when I spent money on business supplies instead of extra snacks or small luxuries for them.

I questioned myself constantly: *Am I selfish? Am I doing too much? Am I even making a difference?* But here's what I also saw:

- My children watching me work hard and knowing what resilience looks like

- My personal confidence growing as I hit small wins - one sale, one client, one breakthrough at a time

- God strengthening me, not when everything was fixed, but while I was still learning, still stretching, still believing

I didn't wait to become "her" once everything was polished. I became "her" in the middle of the fight.

Practical Tools for the Woman in Progress

1. Track Your Wins Weekly- Every Sunday, write down three things you did right… not just what's missing. Small wins build big momentum.

2. Rewrite the Mom Guilt Narrative - Instead of "I missed that moment", say "I am showing my children how to chase purpose, even if it's hard."

3. Stay Anchored to Your "Why" - Money stress is real. But remember: you are investing, not wasting. Every sacrifice is a seed. And seeds take time to grow.

4. Be Gentle With Yourself - Rest when you need. Cry when you need. But don't give up. You're allowed to be a masterpiece and a work in progress at the same time.

HER Moment Journal Prompt

What habits or distractions are robbing me of my freedom? What would my life look like if I honored my time and money more intentionally? What small step can I take this week toward the future I want?

Closing Words

This isn't about grinding. This is about growing.

Discipline isn't here to punish you. It's here to protect you. To position you. To build a bridge between where you are and where you know you're called to be. Every sacrifice you make for your freedom is a seed. And when it blooms, you'll thank the version of you who refused to quit.

"She is no longer the woman who needed to be rescued, she is now the woman who overcame and saved herself."

A Letter to the Woman Becoming Her While Still in Process

Hey you beautiful mess.

Yeah, I said it... and I said it with love.

Because I know exactly what it feels like to be in the in-between. Not who you were, not quite who you're becoming. Trying to break free, but still bound to old patterns. Still checking your bank account like it's a game of roulette. Still battling the voice in your head that says, "You're not ready."

But let me be the one to tell you… you are allowed to become her, even while you're still figuring it out.

You don't have to wait until the debt is gone or until the healing is complete. You don't have to wait until your confidence is unshakable and your house is spotless and your emotions are in perfect balance.

Sis, becoming is messy.

And holy. And beautiful. And really hard sometimes.

I know because I lived it. There were days I poured into my business after crying in the bathroom at work. Nights I lit candles just to remind myself that peace is possible. Mornings I woke up to fight for a future I couldn't fully see yet, but I believed in it anyway. I didn't have it all together; I was just determined not to stay where I was.

Listen to me, love: you can have a vision and still have bad days. You can be building your dream and still be triggered by your past. You can fall apart on Tuesday and show up like a boss on Wednesday.

That's not hypocrisy. That's transformation in real time.

So if no one's told you this lately… you're doing better than you think. And you're not behind. You're just becoming. Give yourself grace. Rest when you need to. But don't you dare quit.

Because the woman you're becoming? She's already proud of you for not giving up here.

Keep building… imperfect, powerful, and in progress.

With every piece of my heart,

Triecia

Chapter Nine

Reclaiming Your Identity Beyond Motherhood and Struggle

"You are fearfully and wonderfully made." - Psalm 139:14

You are more than what you do. You are more than who you care for. You are more than what you've survived.

For so long we've been told:

- You're the strong one

- You're the mother

- You're the wife

- You're the provider

- You're the surviver

But who are you underneath all that? Who are you when nobody is asking for anything? Who are you when you're not producing, performing, proving? We lose ourselves not because we're weak, but because we've been busy holding up the world.

What Reclaiming Your Identity Really Means

It's not about quitting your job. It's not about walking away from your family. It's not about abandoning your responsibilities. It's about remembering:

"I am a woman first. I am a soul first. I am me first - before I am anyone else's anything."

It's giving yourself permission to be:

- Soft when you've been hard

- Playful when you've been serious

- Creative when you've been structured

- Dreamy when you've been practical.

You are allowed to exist for you, not just for what you do for others.

How We Lose Ourselves

We lose ourselves in:

- Caretaking

- Overworking

- Surviving

- Pleasing

- Proving

We start to believe: *"I'll come back to myself later, once the bills are paid, once the kids are grown, once my partner is happy, once the dream is stable."*

But here's the truth: you can't pour from an empty soul. And no one's coming to hand you your identity back. You have to reclaim it.

How to Reclaim Yourself

1. Do something this week just for you - not productive, not perfect, just personal

2. Speak aloud one truth about who you are - not tied to a role or responsibility

3. Notice where you shrink, silence, or sacrifice your voice - and choose to show up a little more boldly.

4. Reconnect with the dreams you put down - write them, name them, honor them

HER Moment Journal Prompt

Who am I underneath my titles, roles, and responsibilities?

What part of me have I been silencing or neglecting?

Closing Words

You are not selfish for wanting more. You are not ungrateful for wanting space to breathe. You are not wrong for remembering you are more than the roles you play. This is your time to return to yourself. Piece by piece. Day by day. Breath by breath.

"She didn't leave her life behind. She simply reclaimed her place inside it."

A letter to the Woman Who Forgot Who She Was

Hey you. Yeah… you, the woman buried under everybody else's needs. The one who answers to "Mom," "Ma," "Mama" and everything in between, but hasn't heard her own name in what feels like forever.

Let me ask you something you probably haven't asked yourself in years:

Who are you… outside of what you do for everybody else?

I know that question stings a little. Because somewhere between late-night bottles, court papers, overtime shifts, and crisis after crisis… you lost her.

The you that used to laugh at dumb rom-coms. The you that used to dance in the mirror with your hairbrush like it was a mic. The you that had dreams so big they scared her. That girl didn't disappear. She just got quiet. It's time to wake her up.

You are more than a mother. More than a survivor. More than the struggle that tried to name you.

Yes, your children are your heart. Yes, you've been through hell and high water. But your identity? It existed before the world demanded so much of you.

And guess what?

You don't need permission to go find her again. Start small. Buy yourself the perfume that makes you feel expensive. Pick up the journal and write like your words matter, because they do. Wear the color that makes you feel seen. Make decisions that honor the woman you're becoming, not just the one who's been surviving.

This chapter of your life? It's not about proving you're strong. We already know you are. This is about remembering you're still a whole woman, worthy, vibrant, alive, even when no one's calling your name but the bills.

Breathe. You are not lost. You're just waiting to be reclaimed. And I promise you this… the version of you that rises from this rediscovery? She's going to blow your own mind.

Now go find her.

With unshakable love,

Triecia

CHAPTER TEN

Breaking Free From Generational Trauma

"Cast all you cares on Him because He cares for you." - 1 Peter 5:7

There comes a moment in every woman's life, especially the strong ones, the tired ones, the ones who've been holding it down for everybody, when she stops mid-step and whispers, "Why do I do it like this? And who taught me I had to?" That moment is sacred. It's the beginning of your freedom. Because generational trauma doesn't always come in the form of abuse or loud dysfunction. Sometimes it's the quiet beliefs, the "normal" habits, the things we never questioned. Sometimes it's passed down as wisdom, but it's really just wounded survival.

Raised by Strength, Starved for Softness

I didn't realize how much I had internalized overworking and emotional silence until I started unraveling as a woman.

Deep in motherhood, trying to chase freedom, and crying in silence while still getting up for work the next morning.

I was raised mostly by my dad, a single Black father in his twenties trying to raise four children, myself and three brothers. He was the constant. He made sure we had what we needed. And when he couldn't do it alone, my aunties and our extended family stepped in.

I now understand the pressure he must have felt... working his main job and doing handy work on the side, providing for four children, carrying a mountain of responsibility on his back. But even with all that love and protection, there wasn't room for emotion.

I didn't see my father cry. I didn't see him pause. I saw strength. I saw sacrifice. I saw hustle. Because in our community, especially for Black men, softness was a threat, not a safe space.

I didn't know it then, but I started modeling that same behavior before I even had a choice. I thought holding everything in was strength. That overworking and staying busy meant you were doing life right. And when it came to softness... gentle affection, emotional nurture, being shown how to be a woman... I struggled.

My mother was in my life, but on the outside looking in, I remember her working hard to maintain her lifestyle. She liked nice things. She always had her hair done, dressed well, and carried herself with confidence. There were things I admired about her, things I still admire now as a woman.

But as a little girl, I often felt like there wasn't space for me in that world. I didn't know how to say it then, but I missed the warmth I saw other girls getting, the nurturing, the softness, the kind of mom who pulled you in and held you when your heart hurt.

I don't say this to cast blame. I know now that she was probably surviving too, in her own way. I know she loved me the way she knew how. But there was a quiet ache that grew in me from that space that wasn't filled.

And it followed me. Into adulthood. Into parenting. Into the way I expected myself to always be okay. I became the woman who didn't cry. The woman who always pushed through. The woman who thought if she worked hard enough, maybe she'd finally feel seen, held, or safe. I thought that was normal. I thought that was strength. But the truth? I was repeating a story that didn't start with me.

And now, I'm learning that just because I was raised by strength doesn't mean I have to live without softness. I can learn to be both. I can be the mother I needed. I can be the woman I never saw. And I can love my parents, and still name the place where I needed more.

How Generational Trauma Hides in Our Lives

It looks like:

- Working until your body breaks down

- Saying "I'm fine" when you're falling apart

- Believing you have to earn rest, love, or joy

- Never asking for help because "strong women don't need anyone"

- Avoiding softness because survival taught you it's dangerous

- Building your entire life around other people's needs and calling it "purpose"

And it sounds like:

- "You better not cry"

- "What happens in this house, stays in this house."

- "You think you're too good for this life?"

- "That's just how it is for woman like us."

But no more. You are not obligated to repeat what broke the woman before you. You are allowed to grieve, to soften, to do things differently - even if no one else understands it yet.

Why It's So Hard to Let Go

We don't just carry their patterns. We carry their pain. Their sacrifices. Their unspoken prayers. Their fears about what could happen if we step outside the box they had to live in. So when we decide to do things differently, whether that means starting a business, resting without guilt, parenting with softness, expressing emotion, or even choosing ourselves, it can feel like betrayal.

But it's not. You are honoring their survival by refusing to live your entire life in survival mode.

Breaking the Cycles: 5 Steps to Healing

1. Name it.

Sit with yourself in honesty. What beliefs, behaviors, and patterns have you carried that didn't start with you?

- Do you overwork to feel worthy?

- Do you shut down emotionally because that's what you saw growing up?

- Do you parent with fear instead of presence?

- Do you keep peace with others while going to war with yourself?

This step takes courage. But naming it gives it a boundary - and boundaries are where healing begins.

Ask yourself: *"What cycle am I still living in that I promised myself I'd break?"*

2. Feel it.

"Grief is a necessary part of growth."

Before you can let go, you have to feel what it cost you to hold on. Maybe you are mourning the childhood you never got, or the woman you were forced to become too soon. Maybe you are grieving the fact that your mother did not know how to love softly, or that your father did not know how to be emotionally present. Maybe you are grieving the woman you could have been if you were not always in survival mode.

Let yourself cry. Yell. Write. Sit in the stillness. Tears are not weakness. They're sacred release. Ask yourself: *"What part of me have I been avoiding because it hurts too much to feel?"*

3. Choose a New Truth.

"What they taught you is not all there is."

After you name it and feel it - you get to rewrite it. You don't need permission to believe something better. Start with one old belief and choose a are one to live by.

Old Belief	*New Truth*
"I have to do it all myself"	"I am worthy of help and support"
"I'm only valuable if I'm useful."	"I am valuable simply because I exist"
"Rest is lazy."	"Rest is a form of respect."
"Strong means silent."	"True strength embraces truth."

Write your new truths. Speak them out loud. Post them on your mirror. Let them become your emotional GPS.

Ask yourself: *"What truth do I want to raise my children on instead?"*

4. Set boundaries without guilt.

"Peace requires protection."

You cannot heal in the same environment that broke you. Whether it's family, friends, old routines, or your own guilt - you are allowed to protect your growth. Setting boundaries doesn't make you mean. It makes you healthy. You don't have to attend every argument you're invited to. You don't have to explain your healing to people committed to misunderstanding you.

Your peace is not up for debate.

Ask yourself: *"Where in my life am I leaking energy because I won't say no?"*

5. Model healing

"Let you life be the lesson."

You don't need a stage, a title, or a huge following to change lives. Just live your healing out loud. Let your children see you say "I'm sorry." Let your friends witness you honoring your no. Let your daughter watch you rest without shame. Let your son hear you talk about your emotions.

You're not just breaking the cycle, you're rebuilding the standard.

Ask yourself: *"What message is my life sending to the people watching me grow?"*

A Letter to the Woman Breaking Free

From one healing woman to another…

Sis,

If you are reading this and your heart feels heavy, I want you to know I see you. I know what it feels like to carry more than your soul was meant to hold. To keep showing up for everyone else while quietly falling apart inside. To wonder if healing is even possible when your wounds have existed longer than your peace.

I have sat in silence after long days, asking God if I was broken or just tired of being strong. Let me tell you something no one may have told you: You are not behind. You are breaking through. You are becoming the woman your younger self dreamed about, and your future self will thank you for.

You are not too late to change the story. You are right on time to begin again. So cry if you need to. Rest when it is heavy. But promise me you will keep going.

Because I need you. Your children need you. The next generation needs the you that is free.

With love,

Triecia

Your sister in strength, softness, and becoming.

Chapter Eleven

The Silent Battles - Guilt, Money, Stress & Comparison

"She was fighting battles no one clapped for. But she kept showing up anyway."

There is a kind of tired you cannot sleep off. It is not just from working or being on your feet all day. It is the weight of trying to hold your household together, heal your heart, chase your dreams, and still make it to parent-teacher conferences with clean clothes and a decent attitude.

It is the kind of exhaustion that comes from being everything to everybody, and still wondering if it is enough.

Let's talk about the battles that do not make it to Instagram. The ones that sit heavy on your chest when the house is quiet. The ones you fight while still cooking dinner, folding laundry, and picking French fries and Cheerios out of the backseat.

Guilt: The Universal Guest That Won't Leave

You feel guilty when you're working late. Guilty when you miss a school event. Guilty for wanting a nap. Guilty for being too nice.

You feel guilty when your child says, "You're always on your computer, Mama." But they don't know you're building a dream that might change both your lives. They don't know you skipped lunch again so they could have field trip money. They don't know you're still grieving the parts of yourself you lost just trying to keep them safe.

This guilt creeps into every moment and makes you feel like no matter how much you do, you're still falling short. But here's what I need you to remember: you are showing up. Even with fear. Even with doubt. Even with empty hands and a tired heart. That counts.

Money Stress: When the Math Ain't Mathing

There is a certain stress that hits when you are five days from payday, the gas light is on, and your child tells you they need supplies for a project due tomorrow.

Have you ever stood in Dollar Tree doing math in your head, pretending to scroll your phone so nobody sees your tears? Have you ever had to say, "Not this week, baby," knowing they have already heard that too many times? Have you ever put something back in the grocery store line and prayed the cashier would not say it out loud?

This kind of stress doesn't just live in your wallet... it lives in your body like knots in your back. The tension in your jaw. The sleep you can't catch. And sometimes, it makes you feel like you're failing. But hear me loud, sis:

You are not irresponsible for wanting more. You are not greedy for dreaming of freedom. And you are not broken because the bills outweigh your paycheck.

You are simply in a chapter where your effort is greater that your income. But that won't always be the case.

Comparison: The Silent Thief

You want to be happy for them... and you are. But part of you is wondering, "How are they making it look so easy?" You see her husband showing up. You see her house spotless. You see her business booming, her kids dressed in matching outfits, and the captions full of joy.

Meanwhile, you are using Afterpay on school shoes. Your house is in survival mode. You have not folded a single load of laundry all week. You don't even know what's for dinner. And worst of all, you are trying your best and still feel like you are behind.

But what you do not see is her behind-the-scenes. The breakdowns. The doubts. The credit card debt. The sleepless nights.

Sis, listen. What God has for you is not late. It is custom-fit just for you. Do not compare your messy middle to someone else's filtered highlight reel.

Let's Be Real

You're not the only person who:

- Cried in your car in the work parking lot

- Didn't answer calls because you had nothing left to give

- Used rewards points just to get coffee or groceries

- Smiled at a birthday party when your heart was breaking

- Laid awake wondering if you'll ever feel free

But you're still here. And every single day, you lace up your faith and fight again.

A Letter to the Woman Who's Tired of Pretending She's Fine

From one soul to another… if you are sitting in the dark, read this slowly.

Hey sis,

I do not have fancy words for you right now. Just real ones. Honest ones. The kind that sit next to your tears and do not rush you to be okay. You are not weak for feeling everything all at once. You are not failing because you are overwhelmed. You are not behind just because it hurts right now.

You are tired... I see that. Tired in your bones. Tired in your spirit. Tired of having to be strong just to survive. You get up every day and push through things no one even knows about. You smile when you want to scream. You give when you are empty. You love even when you feel unseen. And I need you to hear me when I say this is not weakness. That is sacred strength.

You do not need to do more to be worthy. You do not need to fix everything by yourself. You do not need to shrink your dreams or silence your pain. You need rest. You need room to be human. You need to know it is okay to break sometimes, because that is where the rebuilding starts.

Sis, I know it feels like nobody sees you. But God does. I do. And one day, you will look back at this chapter and say, "This is where everything shifted." Keep going, not because you have to prove anything, but because your story is not finished yet. And what is ahead of you is worth every tear, every prayer, every sleepless night, and every broken moment. You do not just deserve peace. You were made for it.

Wipe your face. Fix your crown. Take one more step. You have survived everything that was meant to break you. Now it is your time to build something beautiful from the ashes.

With love,

Triecia

Chapter Twelve

Generational Trauma- The Chains We Didn't Know We Were Wearing

"You are the curse-breaker. The pattern-shifter. The cycle-ender."

You didn't wake up one day with low self-worth, survival instincts, and an anxious need to overachieve. It was passed down, taught silently, modeled quietly, enforced through routine and repetition. Most of us never had anyone sit us down and say, "Here's the generational trauma you've inherited. Let's break it together."

Instead, we grew up:

- Watching our mothers carry the weight of the world without a tear in sight

- Watching fathers bottle everything up and show love through money and actions but not emotions

- Learning that survival was success - joy was optional

We didn't know what it was called. But we lived it.

Silent Rules We Were Taught (That Were Actually Trauma in Disguise)

"Don't talk about what happens in this house."

- So we learned to hide pain, not process it.

"Stop all that crying before I give you something to cry about."

- So we learned to numb emotions and associate vulnerability with punishment.

"Be Strong"

- So we never learned how to ask for help.

"You better not need nobody"

- So we pushed people away and called it independence

"Nobody ever gave me anything, so you'll be fine."

- So we adopted struggle as normal, and viewed abundance with suspicion.

You were trained to survive. To keep your head down, push through, and never complain. But baby - *we're not in survival anymore. We're ready to live.*

Real -Life Examples of Generational Trauma in Action

- A woman who can't accept compliments without deflecting because she was raised in a household where love was earned, not given.

- Mother who yells at her kids for making mistakes - not because she's cruel, but because she grew up being punished harshly and thinks control equals love.

- A grown woman who panics every time she has to spend money, even when she has enough - because she grew up hearing, *"We can't afford that."* On repeat.

- A woman who never speaks up in relationships - because she watched generations of women in her family *"keep the peace"* by keeping quiet.

These are not personality traits. They're trauma responses that have been passed down and repeated like family recipes.

The Pain of Being the First to Say, "This Stops With Me"

When you decide to break the pattern, you become the "difficult one." The "too sensitive one." The one who "thinks she's better." You'll have moments where you wonder:

- *"Am I the problem?"*

- *"Why do I feel so alone?"*

- *"Maybe I should just go back to doing what everyone else does."*

But deep down, you know: You were chosen to start something new. And baby, that's not a punishment - that's purpose.

You're a curse breaker. The chain snapper. The blueprint writer. It's heavy, yes. But the freedom your child will experience because of it? **Unmatched.**

Breaking the Cycle Means

- Choosing therapy even if your family calls it "airing dirty laundry"

- Saying "I love you" to your kids even if you never heard it yourself

- Learning to say "no" without guilt

- Not beating yourself up for resting

- Crying openly in front of your children so they know it's safe to feel

You're not trying to erase your family - you're trying to heal your future.

That Is What Real Legacy Looks Like

You want to leave your kids more than money. You want to leave them:

- Emotional safety

- Space to ask questions without fear

- The ability to say, *"I'm not okay,"* and be met with love

- *Permission to choose peace over pressure*

You are building a new bloodline in real time. And it starts with the decisions you're making today.

Affirmations for the Cycle Breaker

Repeat these when it gets heavy.

When you feel alone.

When you wonder if it's even worth it.

(Spoiler alert: It is.)

- I was born to break what broke generations before me.

- I release guilt, shame and silence - they are not mine to carry

- My healing is not betrayal. My growth is not disrespect.

- I am creating a new legacy, and it starts with my voice.

- I honor where I come from, but I choose where I'm going.

- I am not too emotional. I am finally feeling what others suppressed.

- I don't need permission to protect my peace.

- My future family will inherit love, softness, and freedom - not survival.

- Being the first is hard, but I was chosen for this.

- The chains stop here. The healing begins with me.

Letter to the Cycle Breaker

To the one sitting in the gap, between what was and what will be, this is for you.

Hey love,

I know you are tired. Not just physically, but tired in your bones. Tired of being strong. Tired of always holding it down.

Tired of pretending you are fine when your heart is barely holding on.

You are doing something no one before you dared to do. You are healing what was never healed. You are questioning what was called "normal." You are showing up for your children in ways no one ever showed up for you. That work is quiet. It is heavy. But it is also holy.

You might not get a thank you. You might get resistance. You might even get called difficult, distant, or "too sensitive." But let me tell you what you really are: You are the chosen one. The bridge between pain and peace. The woman your bloodline has been waiting for.

Every time you choose to listen instead of yell.

Every time you pause to breathe instead of repeat.

Every time you love soft, speak gently, and give yourself grace.

You are rewriting your entire family story.

It does not matter who claps for you. What matters is that you are clapping back at the cycles that kept generations stuck. So if you are crying in your car, know this: You are not failing. You are not behind. You are in the middle of breaking something that has been breaking women for decades. That is power. That is purpose. That is legacy. And one day, your children and their children will say, "She is the reason we are free."

Keep going. You are the chain breaker. And the chain stops with you.

With deepest love and highest respect,

Triecia

Chapter Thirteen

Becoming Her - Walking in Purpose on Purpose

"You can't keep pouring from a cup that's cracked at the bottom."

There comes a moment where you stop surviving and start becoming.

Not because everything is perfect. Not because the weight is gone. But because you finally realize that purpose was *never* about perfection… it was about obedience. It was about getting up anyway. It was about letting God use your brokenness to build something holy.

The Myth About Purpose

We think purpose is loud. A platform. A title. A dream car. A fully funded business. But sometimes purpose is:

- Saying "no" when you used to people please

- Raising your children with gentleness you never received

- Starting the business even though you're terrified

- Writing the book, launching the course, posting the video - even when you doubt yourself

- Loving yourself out loud after years of criticizing every inch

Purpose isn't always a spotlight. Sometimes it's a whisper from God saying, *"Keep going... this matters."*

When Purpose Feels Bigger Than You

You may look at your calling and feel unqualified. You might say:

- *"Who am I to do this?"*

- *"What if I mess this up?*

- *"I still have so much healing to do."*

Let me be the one to remind you: God doesn't call the qualified. He qualifies the called. And sis... if you feel it pulling at you...That's not random.That's your assignment.

Your story.

Your struggles.

Your voice.

They were never meant to stay hidden. They are someone else's confirmation that they're not alone.

Becoming "Her" isn't a vibe… It's a War

You are not just waking up one day and glowing up. You are letting go of the woman you were told to be. You are doing scary things. You are disappointing people who were comfortable with your silence. You are losing friends, shifting environments, sacrificing sleep, and questioning everything.

And through all of that, you are still becoming. Still getting dressed. Still praying. Still showing up for your life like you know God has you even when you cannot see it yet. This is the work. This is the walk.

Your Purpose May Be Connected to Your Pain

The enemy tried to break you in the same place God plans to bless others through you.

If your pain was around motherhood, your purpose might be tied to helping other moms. If you struggled with identity, your purpose might be helping women rediscover theirs. If you have been financially stuck, your purpose might include teaching wealth, building strategies, or starting businesses.

Your purpose is often hidden in your testimony. And baby, you got receipts.

So, Where Do You Start?

Right. Where. You. Are.

- Start the business with the knowledge you already have

- Write the blog post with your trembling hands

- Record the podcast from your car

- Post the content, write the caption, launch the idea.

- Host the class, lead the room, pray the prayer.

There is no perfect time. There's just right now. And you are more ready than you think.

Affirmations for the Woman Stepping Into Her Purpose

Say them out loud. Say them trembling. Say them anyway.

- I am walking in my purpose, on purpose.

- What I carry is valuable. What I've survived is powerful.

- I may not feel ready, but I am already equipped.

- I trust the God in me to lead me, even through fear.

- I will not shrink to make others comfortable.

- I am becoming the woman I once prayed to be.

- Every step I take is aligned with my calling.

- I no longer wait for permission… I create the path.

- I can rest and still be chosen. I can rise and still be soft.

- I am HER… not someday, but now.

Letter to the Woman on the Edge of Her Becoming

To the one staring at the dream, heart racing, knees shaking… this is for you.

Hey love,

I see you. On the edge of something so big it scares you. Holding your breath, holding your ideas, holding your tears. You are standing between who you have been and who you are becoming, and I know how heavy that in-between can feel.

But I need you to know this: You do not have to be perfect to be powerful. You do not have to have it all figured out to start. You just have to move, even if it is trembling, even if it is slow.

Purpose rarely shows up with a blueprint. It often arrives disguised as a burden, a whisper, or a holy nudge that will not let you sleep at night. The thing in your belly, the dream you keep silencing, the idea you keep pushing to the back burner... that is not random. That is divine.

You were chosen to disrupt cycles, to create change, to show other women that it is possible to rise from anything. And I know you are scared. You do not want to fail. You do not want to be seen starting from the bottom. But sis, every woman you admire once stood exactly where you are now... scared but faithful, unsure but obedient.

You are not behind and you are not too late. You are right on time, and you are more capable than you realize. So take the step. Write the post. Launch the business. Say yes to what sets your soul on fire, because on the other side of this fear is the freedom you have been craving. And trust me, once you say yes to purpose, life will never be the same again.

You got this. You always did.

With all my belief in you,

Triecia

Chapter Fourteen

You Deserve Nice Things - Breaking the Scarcity Mindset

"The Lord is my shepherd; I shall not want." Psalm 23:1

There is a phrase I hear too often from women, especially single mothers:

"I can't afford that."

"That's not for people like me."

"One day, when things get better…"

Sis, let me tell you something that may shake you. You do not have to earn the right to want more. You are allowed to want joy, softness, beauty, and peace, even in the middle of the storm.

This chapter is not just about buying things. It is about believing you deserve them. It is about undoing the lie that you have to struggle endlessly before you can experience ease.

Where Scarcity Mindset Comes From

We weren't born thinking small. We were taught it. We saw:

- Mothers robbing Peter to pay Paul

- Generations saying "as long as the lights are on, we're fine"

- Celebrations and events skipped because "money's tight"

- Dreams placed on pause so survival could take the front seat

And now we say:

- "I don't need it, I'll just make do."

- "I'll get something for the kids, not for me."

- "Maybe next year."

But the truth is, you've been deferring joy so long you forgot what it feels like. You've made struggle your home. And now it's time to evict that mindset.

Real Talk: Scarcity Shows Up Like This:

- You feel guilty spending money on yourself

- You don't trust that more money will come back to you

- You constantly say, *"I can't afford it,"* without even checking your options

- You underprice your services or avoid charging at all

- You're always waiting for *"One day"* before you enjoy anything.

Let me lovingly say this:

You can't step into overflow while clinging to "barely enough."

But What if You Really Are Struggling?

I'm not here to sell you fantasy.

There are bills, rent, kids, and real-life pressure.

But what I am here to do is help you:

1. Shift your perspective

2. Stretch your resources

3. Save for the life you deserve

Let's talk about what you can do now - no extra income required.

Simple, Small Ways to Start Saving for What you Deserve

1. Create a "Nice Things" Fund - Even if it's $5 a Week

Put in a labeled envelope or a digital savings folder. Name it boldly:

- "New Couch Fund"

- "Business Start-Up"

- "Solo Date Money"

- "Dream Trip 2026"

It's not about the amount - it's about the *intention.*

2. Cut One Thing That Doesn't Serve You

Audit your spending. Cancel one subscription you don't use. Stop impulse buying snacks. Pause the fast food. Then reroute that money to your "Nice Things" or "business fund."

3. Use the "Three - Day Rule"

Before making any emotional purchases, wait 3 days. Still want it? Great. Don't? You saved coins. Now apply that to sales, launches, and services. Trust me… you'll see how much you were reacting and not planning.

4. Sell Something You Don't Use

Old electronics, clothes, furniture. You might have a blessing sitting in the closet. Use that extra cash to buy something meaningful or fund your first supply order.

5. Start a Dream Jar with Your Kids

Make it a family thing. Let them learn early that *we save for what we want.* You're not just building a habit - you're building a legacy.

Real Life Example: From "I Can't" to "I Did"

There was a time I felt ashamed for not being able to afford nice candles, and now I make and sell them. I remember skipping meals to stretch for gas but still setting aside $20 to buy jars and fragrance oil. Was it easy? No. But I made a decision: I would no longer let temporary struggle dictate my permanent mindset.

And every time I lit one of those candles, I remembered:

"I created this. I deserve to feel good. Even now."

Mindset Reframes That Changed Everything

Instead of: *"I can't afford that."*

Try: *"How can I make this happen?"*

Instead of: *"I'll never have enough."*

Try: *"I'm learning to manage what I have better while preparing for more."*

Instead of: *"It's too late for me."*

Try: *"I'm right on time for my next season."*

Affirmations for Breaking the Scarcity Mindset

Repeat these slowly. Speak them until they feel true. Let them break every lie lack every told you.

- I am no longer available for a mindset of lack.

- I am worthy of joy, ease, and overflow.

- Money is not my master... it is my tool.

- I deserve softness and abundance, even while Im still healing.

- I can be responsible with money and still enjoy nice things.

- Saving is an act of self-respect. Spending wisely is an act of self-love.

- My desires are not selfish. They are a signal for what's possible.

- I don't have to shrink to be safe - I am safe to expand.

- Every dollar I steward today is preparing me for increase.

- Wealth is not just for them. It's for me too

Letter to the Woman Afraid to Want More

To the woman who whispers "I can't afford that" louder than she speaks her dreams, this is for you.

Hey sis,

You have spent so long being "realistic" that you forgot how to be hopeful. You have been calculating bills in your head while smiling through the pain. You have convinced yourself that other women get luxury, peace, and pretty things… but you? You are just trying to keep the lights on.

Let me stop you right there. You deserve more. Not because you have worked yourself into the ground but simply because you are worthy. I know you were taught to make do, to stretch every dollar until it begged for mercy. To deny yourself until there was nothing left to want.

But here's what I need you to understand:

Wanting more doesn't make you ungrateful… it makes you aware.

Aware that peace does not only come on payday. Aware that your kids deserve vacations and you deserve moments of joy.

Aware that maybe… just maybe… you were not meant to live in survival mode forever.

Sis, abundance is not a fantasy. It is a mindset first and then a reality. And yes, it starts small. Skipping that twelve-dollar fast food run to buy your first candle supplies. Putting five dollars in your "dream fund" and smiling like it is five hundred. Choosing to believe that this is the season things start shifting.

You do not have to wait until you are debt-free to enjoy your life. You do not have to earn softness with exhaustion. You do not need permission to pursue comfort, beauty, or ease. Let this be the last time you say, "I can't afford that" without asking, "But what if I could?"

Start where you are. Make room in your life and in your mind for the possibility of more. Because sis, the soft life is not a luxury. It is your birthright.

With all the love and belief in your next chapter,

Triecia

Chapter Fifteen

Your Environment Matters - When Chaos Moves in and Peace Moves out

"A cluttered space is often the cry of a cluttered mind."

There's a certain kind of heartbreak that comes from looking around your home and feeling defeated.

It's the kind of heartbreak that doesn't cry loudly; it just sighs deeply. You walk from room to room, overwhelmed by everything you haven't done yet. You know it's not supposed to look like this, but every time you want to fix it, your body says, "Not today… I'm too tired."

And before you know it, weeks have passed. The house looks how you feel inside—unkept, unattended, and tired.

This Isn't About Changing. This Is About Capacity

Let's get honest.

You didn't let the house go because you're lazy. You let the house go because you were barley holding yourself together.

- The pile of laundry? That's the weight you've been carrying.

- The dishes in the sink? That's the stuff you've had to swallow.

- The cluttered table? That's the chaos in your mind you've had to quiet.

Every item out of place is a symptom of emotional exhaustion. You're tired of begin tired. Tired of keeping up. Tired of pretending like it's all ok... when it's isn't.

When You're the Only One Holding It All

Nobody tells you how heavy it is when the house depends on you. When the kids do not clean up after themselves. When nobody else sees the mess but you. When you do not even have the energy to ask for help. You want to rest... but how can you rest when there is always something needing attention?

So you just collapse. Not from laziness, but from trying to be everything, every day, for everyone.

The Candle That Reminded Me I Deserved Peace

I will never forget that night. Shoes were scattered by the door like they had been kicked off mid-chaos. My counters were cluttered with things I had meant to put away days ago. The bathroom mirror had tiny fingerprints, and I was too tired to even be annoyed. The air felt heavy, not because of noise, but because of everything I had not said out loud.

But I walked into the kitchen, pulled out one of my candles, and lit it. The house did not magically become peaceful. But in that one small flicker, something shifted inside me. I sat down, and for the first time that day, I did not do anything else. I did not fold a thing. Did not wipe anything. Did not answer a single text. I just stared at that flame... and finally let myself exhale.

That moment was my turning point. Not because the space was clean - it wasn't. Not because life was perfect - far from it. But because I realized:

"Even in the mess... I still get to have peace. I still get to want more. I still get to choose me."

That one candle became more than just a scent in the room. It became a symbol of my right to heal. Of my softness. Of my comeback. And eventually... It sparked the dream that became my business. All from one flame, one pause, one breath in the middle of the chaos.

Let's Talk About the Guilt

You ever feel guilty for:

- Letting the house go?

- Not cleaning before bed?

- Letting your kids eat cereal for dinner?

- Closing the door on a room you don't have enough energy to clean?

Let me speak truth to you:

You are not a failure.

You are a woman carrying more than most people know. And even if the house isn't spotless, you're still creating a home with your love, your laughter, your sacrifice. But you also deserve peace, too. You deserve a space that reflects the softness you crave, even if it starts with just one clean chair, one fresh sheet, one prayer whispered over a mop.

Shifting Your Space Without Shame.

You don't have to wait for motivation. You need movement. Gentle. Intentional. Small. Here's how you start:

1. Reclaim One Corner

Pick a space that feels sacred. Your nightstand, your prayer chair, the bathroom sink. Clear it. Wipe it down. Add something beautiful - even if it's just a folded towel or a handwritten note to yourself.

2. Create a "No Chaos" Zone

Designate one room or section that must stay peaceful. It could be your bedroom or a single chair. Train your mind: *this is my calm place.*

3. Clear Clutter With Compassion

If it's been sitting there for weeks, it doesn't mean you're lazy. It means you've been overwhelmed. Forgive yourself and clear it piece by piece.

4. Invite Peace in With Intention

Light a candle. Play soft music. Open the blinds. Spray your favorite scent (Like a Serenity 920 room spray). Say out loud: *"Peace lives here now."*

Creating Softness on a Budget

Softness doesn't cost much. But it changes everything.

Try this:

- $1 candles from Dollar Tree

- Rearranging your space for better flow

- A handwritten affirmation taped to the wall

- Free Youtube playlist for calming music

- A $5 journal from Walmart that holds your whole heart

You don't need a new home to have a new atmosphere. You need a new approach to your own worth.

Affirmations for the Woman Trying to Heal in Chaos

Repeat these softly. Loudly. In your head and in your heart. With your eyes closed or standing in a mess that doesn't define you.

- I am not my mess - I am worthy of peace, even in the middle of it.

- Every breath I take is a step toward clarity, calm, and control.

- My home is shifting because I am shifting.

- I release shame, and I make room for softness.

- I deserve a space that reflects my healing, not just my hustle.

- One corner at a time, I am realizing my peace.

- Even if everything isn't perfect - I am still progressing.

A letter to the Woman Drowning in Her Own Space

Hey love,

I know you are tired. Not just "I need a nap" tired, but soul tired. The kind of tired where even thinking about cleaning feels like a mountain you do not have the strength to climb. I see the shoes at the door. The piles you have walked past for days. The rooms you have avoided because walking into them feels like one more reminder that you are "not enough." But you are.

You are enough, even when your house is not spotless. You are worthy, even when your to-do list stays unchecked. You are doing beautifully, even when everything around you feels undone. This is not your forever. This is your pause. You have every right to be overwhelmed. You have been carrying weight most people do not even notice. But I want you to hear me when I say this: *You do not need a clean house to deserve a calm heart.*

Light that candle. Sit down, even if the laundry isn't folded. Breathe deeply, even if dinner isn't cooked. Play your favorite song, even if the living room is a mess. This is the work of healing... choosing peace when you've been trained for pressure. One small corner. One breath. One new belief at a time.

And just in case no one's said it lately: I'm proud of you. You are not behind. You are becoming. And your home - just like your heart - is learning how to hold peace again.

With Love,

Me, your sister in the fight for softness

Triecia

Chapter Sixteen

Letting Go of the Woman You Were Told to Be

"Do not conform to the pattern of this world, but be transformed by the renewing of your mind." - Romans 12:2

Hey Sis,

I need you to stop for a minute. Put the weight down. Close the tabs in your mind. Let this moment be just for you. Because I see you. Trying so hard to be the woman you were told you had to be. The one who never says no. The one who is always put together. The one who carries the house, the kids, the job, the secrets… all without falling apart. But what if I told you that you do not have to keep doing that? What if I told you it is safe to let her go?

You Were Taught Survival, Not Softness

You did not choose this version of womanhood. It was handed to you. Passed down by tired mommas and aunties who meant well but did not have the tools. Shaped by a society that told you your worth is in how much you can endure. Formed by relationships that praised your sacrifices but never your softness.

You were taught to:

- Hustle hard

- Stay quiet

- Be strong

- Never need too much

- Never ask too often

And because you're a fighter, you did it. You became her. The woman who gets it done, no matter what it cost.

But I want you to ask yourself something real right now:

Is she making you happy… or just making you tired?

She's Not the Enemy…But She Can't Come With You

The woman you were told to be isn't evil. She's a warrior. She helped you survive some dark nights. But now you're being called into more, and she doesn't fit where you're going.

She still wants to prove herself. You want to free yourself. She still wants to be liked. You want to be whole. She still needs validation. You just want peace.

So it's okay to thank her, and then lovingly let her go.

Best Friend to Best Friend: You Don't Owe Them That Version Anymore

Listen to me carefully- You are *allowed* to stop being the version of yourself that makes other people comfortable.

You are allowed to:

- Change your mind

- Set boundaries

- Say no without guilt

- Rest without earning it

- Dream out loud

- Want Luxury, softness, and freedom

You are not selfish. You are not crazy. You're not doing too much. You're just finally becoming you - and not everybody's going to understand that.

But guess what? You'll survive their opinions. And you'll thrive in your truth.

Let's Burn the Rule Book

You know the one. The one that says you have to have the house clean, a full schedule, and a smile plastered on your face at all times.

Rip it up, sis.

Make your own rules now. Let your womanhood be defined by joy, healing, ease, and honesty. You are not here to prove anything. You are here to live fully, boldly, and beautifully... even if nobody claps.

Start Here, Friend

If you're wondering where to begin, start small:

- Say no when you mean it.

- Rest before you break.

- Speak up when your heart shakes.

- Put on your favorite lipgloss just because.

- Write your own definition of what kind of woman you want to be.

And most importantly? Be okay with being misunderstood while you grow.

Because This is Your Becoming Season

You are not behind. You are just not performing anymore. You are shedding skin. You are walking out of old identities. You are choosing you, and that is the most powerful thing a woman can ever do.

So keep going. Keep showing up. Keep marching to the beat of your own drum, even if the rhythm is brand new. You were not created to fit into their mold. You were born to break it.

Affirmations for the Woman Finally Choosing Herself

- I am no longer performing, I am becoming.

- I release the version of me created for their comfort.

- I am allowed to change, grow, and redefine myself at any time.

- There expectations do not determine my identity.

- I am whole, even then I choose rest over hustle.

- I choose authenticity over approval.

- The woman I am becoming is rooted in truth, softness, and freedom.

- I am enough... even when I am not everything for everyone.

A Letter to the One Who's Done Performing

Hey Love,

You have been holding your breath for a long time.

Trying to be everything they said you should be. Trying to keep it all together. Trying to make everyone proud, even when it cost you your peace. I know you are tired. Tired of pretending. Tired of shrinking yourself so others could be comfortable.

But sis, you do not have to keep doing that. You do not have to keep wearing the version of you that was built by pressure and survival. You do not have to keep showing up in a role you never auditioned for. You do not have to be strong every second of every day.

You get to be soft. You get to be still. You get to want more.

And the woman you are becoming? She is finally free. So take the mask off and lay down the weight to walk boldly in your truth. You do not need their approval to start your healing. You just need permission, and you already have it.

I love you. I see you. And I am cheering for the real you.

With all the softness and strength,

Triecia

Chapter Seventeen

Becoming Her

"The moment I stopped surviving and started believing, everything changed."

The Moment You Stop Waiting and Start Walking.

You have cried the tears. You have torn off the labels they placed on you. You have sat in your truth until it no longer scared you. Now it is time. Not to prove. Not to impress. But to become Her.

The woman you have been praying to become. The woman who carries peace even in the middle of chaos. The one who no longer asks for permission. The one who chose herself and never looked back.

Becoming her is not a single moment. It is a movement. A decision. A daily walk.

Becoming HER means...

- She's done performing. She shows up honest, raw and real.

- She's done apologizing. She no longer shrinks to be digestible.

- She no longer ignores herself. Her needs matter. Her voice is valid.

- She doesn't hustle for worth. She knows she was born with it.

- She doesn't wait for things to calm down to find peace… she creates it.

- She walks with God, not guilt.

- She speaks life into other woman because she no longer sees them as competition.

Real Talk: Becoming HER Costs Something

It costs:

- Old version of you that were rooted in fear

- Relationships that only loved your brokenness

- Comfort zones that kept you "safe" but stuck

- The illusion that you can do it all without healing

But it returns:

- Power

- Peace

- Purpose

- Alignment

- Confidence

- Legacy

So yeah… it's worth it

What Shifted Everything for Me

It was not some fancy course. It was not a big break or a sudden blessing. It was a breakdown.

I was sitting in my garage, door closed, heart shattered, hoodie sleeves soaked from wiping tears I could not hold back anymore. Everything felt like it was falling apart, but deep down, something in me knew God was doing something. I thought I was being punished, but now I know He was isolating me to work on me.

That was my turning point.

I was tired of surviving. I was also tired of being the strong one. I was tired of showing up for a life that did not feel like mine. So I started small. I lit a candle, picked up my journal, and cried my truth onto the page. I began investing in my business with whatever I had left after paying bills, no return in sight, only faith. I sacrificed sleep and comfort because my freedom mattered more. I stopped waiting for permission. I stopped asking for a better life and started building one.

That was the moment I realized:

Becoming HER wasn't about becoming someone new. It was about finally coming home to the woman I was always meant to be.

Now, it's your turn.

Sis, your shift may not look like mine, but I know you've had your own garage moment, or you will. That breaking point is not the end; it's the invitation.

The invitation to release the version of you that was built by survival and to step boldly into the woman who was built for purpose.

She's in there.

She's always been in there.

You don't have to become her overnight, but you do have to decide. Because the shift doesn't come when life gets easier, it comes when you get clearer about who you are and what you deserve.

And once you choose her, really choose her, life will never be the same.

Affirmations for the Woman Who Refuses to Settle

- I am no longer waiting to be chosen... I choose me.

- I release the version of myself created to survive and I embrace the woman I was created to be.

- Every sacrifice I've made is planting seeds for the life I deserve.

- I am worthy of rest, softness, freedom, and joy - without guilt.

- I honor my journey, but I refuse to stay stuck in who I used to be.

- Peace is my new home, Purpose is my new compass.

- I don't need approval... I need alignment.

- Becoming HER is not a destination, it's a daily decision... and today I say yes.

A Letter to the Woman Who's Ready to Become HER

Hey sis,

Look at you.

Still standing. Still breathing. Still here. Even after everything life threw at you. Even after the silent nights, the long days, and the moments you thought you could not take another step. I know you have been carrying so much... the dreams, the disappointments, the weight of other people's expectations, and the secret fear that maybe, just maybe, you will never become the woman you know you are meant to be.

But let me say this loud and clear, straight from my soul to yours:

You are HER. Right now. Today.

Not just when you hit your goals. Not just when you finally get the house, the income, the peace. But in this moment, raw, real, and unfiltered, you are already becoming.

You do not need to be more. You just need to believe more. Because the moment you believe that HER is already inside of you, everything shifts. The way you walk. The way you talk. The way you protect your peace.

You will stop hustling for validation and start moving in alignment. You will stop playing small and start showing up with authority. And the woman you have been hiding inside for years will finally come out—bold, soft, fierce, healed, and whole.

So here is my prayer for you:

That you will stop doubting.

That you will stop dimming.

That you will stop dragging old versions of yourself into a future that is begging for your truth.

I hope you walk out of this chapter and straight into your power. You are HER. You have always been HER. Now it is time to live like it.

I am rooting for you.

Always,

Triecia

Chapter Eighteen

Let the Legacy Begin

"Once you meet the healed version of yourself, you can't unknow her."

You're Not Just Becoming HER... You're Becoming a Legacy

Somewhere in the middle of it all—the diapers, the debt, the depression, the deadlines—you stopped and asked, *"Is this all there is to life?"* And the answer is no. This is not all there is. This is just where it starts.

You did not survive all that pain, confusion, isolation, and pressure just to stay the same.

You were called for more. You were chosen to shift something. You were anointed to break what others refuse to even acknowledge.

You did not just read this book. You walked through fire. You stared down your fears. You peeled off the mask. You met yourself.

And now… you lead.

Legacy Doesn't Start Later. It Starts Right Now

We think legacy begins when we have made it. When the bank account is full. When the business is booming. When the kids are grown and grateful. When the house is calm and the schedule is clear.

But let me tell you something… legacy starts in the mess.

It starts when you decide to change your mindset even while the bills are stacked. It starts when you take your first step, even with shaky legs. It starts when you teach your children emotional safety, even if you were never taught it yourself.

It starts when you say: *"The chaos ends with me."*

To the Woman Who's Still in the Middle

You are still healing, still juggling, and still unsure. But guess what? You are still her. You don't need the perfect plan. You don't even need to be ready or have every piece in place. You just need to believe that your life is still usable, even with the bruises, the stretch marks, the trauma, and even the heartbreak. Even with the pieces you are still picking up.

God doesn't need perfection to begin the legacy. He needs your yes.

You're the Chain Breaker. The Lineage Shifter.

You are the first in your family to:

- Choose healing over hiding

- Choose therapy over silence

- Choose boundaries over burnout

- Choose softness over survival

- Choose purpose over pretending

You are the woman your bloodline has been waiting for.

You are showing your children that motherhood doesn't not mean martyrdom. You are showing your community that single mothers are powerful, not pitiful. You are showing other women that a comeback is still possible... no matter how far gone it feels.

What Legacy Looks Like in Real Life

- It's choosing a calm "No" instead of an anxious "Yes"

- It's starting a business from your kitchen table after putting the kids to sleep.

- It's deciding to rest on Sunday and honor your soul.

- It's being present - not perfect- with your children.

- It's breaking silence in a family that never talked about feelings.

- It's journaling and praying when everyone is numbing out.

- It's letting yourself be seen, even when you don't feel like enough.

Legacy doesn't always look like a monument. Sometimes, it looks like a woman whispering, *"I'm doing the best I can...and that's enough today."*

You're Not Just Becoming HER... You're Becoming the Wave.

The shift you made will ripple through your family, your friendships, and your future. The kids are watching. Your community is watching. Heaven is watching. And I promise you... what you build will bless more than just you.

You are no longer living just to get by. You are living to create impact. You are living to create freedom. You are living to create a new normal.

And you do not have to wait for the right time. *You are the right time*. Right now is enough. Right now is sacred. Right now is your start.

Affirmations: I Am the Legacy

- I am the first of many. The cycle breaker. The lineage shifter. The legacy.

- I don't wait for the future to find me... I create it, step by step.

- My healing is creating freedom for generations I may never meet.

- Even in the middle of my mess, I am building something that matters.

- God trusted me with this life because he knew I'd do something sacred with it.

- I lead with love. I walk in purpose. I leave behind light.

- The life I'm building is bigger than me... and I'm ready for it.

They Chose HER Too

A Short Story Inspired by the Lives of Women Who Got Tired of Surviving

Brielle hadn't meant to cry at the red light. She blinked quickly, trying to stop the tears from falling before her lashes gave her away. Her son was in the backseat singing off-key to the same Cocomelon song he'd played three hundred times that week, and her daughter had just dropped a chip bag that exploded across the car floor like it was mocking her chaos.

She gripped the steering wheel tighter. The light turned green, but she didn't move right away. Cars honked. She finally hit the gas. This was life lately. Always moving. Always tired. Always barely holding it together.

Brielle was a single mom working a job that drained her, raising two kids with more energy than she could keep up with, and trying to build a candle business from her tiny kitchen counter between loads of laundry. She was burnt out—not the cute kind of "need a spa day" tired, but the bone-deep kind where your body shows up while your soul checks out. The kind where you forget you're a person.

That afternoon, she was late picking her kids up. Again.

She walked into the school's front office, heart racing with the familiar shame of being the last mom to arrive. Her daughter sat in a plastic chair, swinging her feet and trying not to look disappointed. Another mom stood across the room, clearly also having a day—shoes mismatched, bun unraveling, shirt stained with something she had clearly given up fighting.

Their eyes met. A shared nod.

"Rough day?" Brielle asked.

The woman chuckled. "Is there another kind?"

They both laughed. That tired, heavy mom laugh that says, *I feel you.*

"I'm Jasmine," she said. "Single mom of two. Working, barely surviving. You?"

"Brielle," she replied. "Same."

They walked out together and ended up standing in the parking lot for forty-five minutes, trading stories about late bills, forgotten field trip money, dreams they didn't have time for, and the ache of feeling like no one saw them beyond what they did for everyone else.

By the end of the conversation, Jasmine said, "I don't know why, but I feel like I needed this. Like God knew I needed someone who gets it."

Brielle smiled. "Me too."

A few weeks later, they started a little routine. Once a week, after the kids were asleep, they'd FaceTime or meet up at Brielle's apartment. Nothing fancy. Just peace. Jasmine would bring her journal. Brielle would light one of her test candles. Her current scent was lavender and something that smelled like hope.

They called it their *Soft Reset Night.*

"I've been lighting a candle every night," Jasmine said one evening. "It reminds me that I'm allowed to have peace, even in a messy house."

Brielle nodded. "And journaling reminds me I still have a voice, even if I've been silent."

They didn't need answers. They just needed each other.

Monique

Monique entered their lives at a mandatory team-building event Brielle had to attend for work. Jasmine tagged along for moral support and free wine. Monique was upper management. She was polished, calm, and probably wearing perfume that cost more than Brielle's light bill.

But something in Monique's eyes gave her away.

When the three of them ended up in a corner of the room laughing about awkward icebreakers, Brielle caught it—that flicker of tired behind the gloss.

Later, over drinks, Monique said quietly, "I know I don't look it, but I'm exhausted. I'm building a YouTube channel in secret. My husband wants to start a family, but I'm terrified of losing myself. I want freedom before I have kids. But I feel guilty for even wanting that."

Silence. Then Jasmine leaned in. "Sis, you don't have to explain that to us. We get it."

From that moment, something clicked. Three different women. Same storm. Same fight for HER.

Becoming Together

They started meeting up on a regular basis. Sharing resources. Celebrating each other's small wins.

When Brielle finally sold out her first candle batch, they screamed on FaceTime. When Jasmine booked her first therapy session, they cried happy tears. When Monique posted her first lifestyle vlog after months of fear, they flooded the comments.

They weren't just surviving anymore. They were becoming.

And in the middle of bills, kids, jobs, and chaos, they had each other.

Part 2:
The Shift, The Storm, and the Sisterhood

Jasmine's Breaking Point

The apartment was still and quiet, too quiet.

The only sound came from the humming fridge and the occasional creak of the ceiling, like the building itself was exhausted. Jasmine sat slouched at her sticky kitchen table, elbows propped up, face buried in her palms.

It was after midnight. There were no tears yet, just stillness and pressure, like her entire life was pressing on her chest. A crusted bowl of macaroni and cheese sat beside her laptop, still open on a tab titled *"How to Start a Side Hustle with No Money."* Her son's shoes lay by the front door, one untied and flattened, like even the shoes had given up.

The kids were asleep, finally. She should have been in the shower, or asleep herself, or folding the laundry that had become a permanent structure on the couch. But she couldn't move. Her limbs were heavy. Her spirit, even heavier.

She didn't want to die.

She just didn't want to keep living like this.

The guilt crept in first. *Why can't you just get it together like other moms?*

Then came the shame. *You're failing your kids again.*

And just like that, the flood came. Hot, angry, ugly tears spilled down her face and into her hoodie sleeves. She didn't just cry, she broke. Her shoulders trembled, her body rocked back and forth like she could shake herself free from the weight she carried.

Her phone buzzed. She didn't even look at it at first, but it kept buzzing. Finally, she glanced at the screen.

BRIELLE: *"You ok, Suga? Something's telling me to check on you."*

She stared at the message, lips trembling, then typed:

JASMINE: *"I'm not. I think I'm losing it. And I don't think anybody sees me."*

A few minutes passed. Then her doorbell rang.

She wiped her face, pushed herself up on weak knees, and cracked the door open.

Brielle stood there in a hoodie, holding two spicy chicken sandwiches from Popeyes, a bag of fries, and a bottle of cheap wine. Her eyes were soft, full of understanding, no judgment, just love.

"I didn't know what to bring," she said quietly. "So I brought carbs and comfort."

Jasmine broke down again, this time into arms that didn't let her fall.

Monique's Quiet War

Monique sat at the marble kitchen island she once dreamed of having, sipping on tea that had long gone cold. Her husband was in the next room, headphones on, watching a podcast about investments and sports and all the things he believed were building a life.

She stared at her phone screen. The same video she'd recorded weeks ago was paused on a frame where her smile looked strained, her eyes slightly glassy. She had been forcing it, again.

She started her YouTube channel in secret. She called it *Modern & Monique*. It was supposed to be a space where she shared routines, self-care, and femininity—how to be soft yet ambitious, stylish yet grounded. But so far, all it documented was fear. She hadn't posted a single thing.

"I want to wait until it's perfect," she told herself. But deep down, she knew what it really was. She was scared. Scared that people would laugh. Scared her husband would tell her it wasn't real work. Scared her coworkers would roll their eyes. Scared that she'd look ridiculous for wanting more.

That night, she sat on the bathroom floor, knees pulled to her chest, sobbing into a plush towel like it could muffle the sound of her dreams colliding with her reality. When she finally came out, her husband didn't even notice she'd been gone for nearly forty-five minutes.

She opened her Notes app and typed:

"I want a soft life. But I'm scared to ask for it out loud."

Then she clicked on the video, adjusted the thumbnail, and hit *Upload.*

Her hands trembled, but for the first time in months, her spirit felt steady.

Brielle's breakdown & The Candle That Reminded Her

The apartment was quiet but it wasn't peaceful.

Brielle stood in the middle of the living room and saw her overwhelm staring back at her in the mess, in the shoes scattered across the floor, in the pile of laundry that had moved from the couch to the floor and back again for four days straight. The sink was full of dishes. The garbage needed to go out. The hallway smelled like old McDonald's and Bath and Body Works, a scent battle no one was winning.

Bridget had just thrown a tantrum over a missing Barbie shoe. Her son had scribbled crayon all over the dining room wall. Her body was screaming for rest. She just needed a break.

But rest felt like laziness, and lazy, in her world, wasn't allowed.

She picked up a candle from her product shelf, one she hadn't sold, one she'd meant to save for herself. Vanilla Cashmere and White Amber. She lit it without thinking and sat on the floor as the scent wrapped around her like a warm hug. The flame flickered, and in the quiet, it seemed to whisper to her, *You deserve softness too.*

She cried. Soft at first, then deep. She cried for all the things she hadn't said, all the help she didn't ask for, and all the moments she smiled when she wanted to scream.

And when her daughter came and sat beside her, Brielle pulled her close and whispered, "Mommy's tired. But I'm trying. I'm really trying."

The Conversation That Changed Everything

Later that night, all three women sat together... tired, tear-streaked, but whole. Candles lit. Journals open. Music low. Jasmine looked up and said, "I'm realizing it's not just about becoming HER. It's about forgiving the version of me that forgot she mattered."

Monique added, "And shedding the version that only existed to be what everyone else needed."

Brielle wiped her eyes and whispered, "Every day we choose HER… is a day we remember that surviving is not the goal. Living is."

They sat in silence. Not the awkward kind, but the kind that feels like healing. And they pinky promised, like little girls who still believed in magic:

"We choose HER. Again and again. Until choosing HER becomes natural."

They Chose HER Too

Part 3:
Becoming Her, Out Loud

It didn't happen overnight. They didn't wake up healed. The didn't suddenly have five figures in the bank or peace in every corner their lives. But they chose different. Little by little. Day by day. And the ripple effect? Unstoppable.

Jasmine's Freedom Budget

Jasmine started with a notebook from Dollar Tree. She labeled the front: "Freedom Starts Here." She wrote down every bill, every dollar, every habit… even the DoorDash orders and Target runs she "forgot" to mention. It hurt to look at. But she needed to face the truth before she could fix it.

With Brielle's help, she found $80 worth of small cuts in her budget. Then she created a "Freedom Jar." It was literally a glass jar she kept on top of her fridge. She put in every extra dollar she could, no matter how small. One month later, she used that jar to pay off her overdraft and buy supplies to start her side hustle: handmade affirmation keychains. She made seven sales in one week.

It wasn't about the money—not yet. It was about proving to herself that she could start.

She looked at her kids and whispered,

"Mommy's gonna be okay. I promise."

Monique's Moment of Truth

Monique finally told her husband. They were sitting in the car after church, and she couldn't keep the words inside anymore.

"I'm building something, babe. I know it doesn't make sense to you yet, but I need to try. I need to know I didn't abandon my dreams just to play it safe."

He sighed, rubbed his face, and said, "I just don't want to lose you."

She reached for his hands. "You won't. But if I lose myself, we both lose."

It wasn't easy after that. They argued, cried, and circled the same fears over and over. But she didn't stop. She posted videos every week. She started networking. She learned editing, SEO, and brand outreach.

Then one night, her subscriber count hit 1,000. And her husband brought home flowers. "Congrats, baby. I see you."

That was the night she finally started seeing herself too.

Brielle's First Vendor Table

It was a small pop-up shop in a church parking lot. Fold-out tables, hand fans, gospel music, and aunties selling everything from oils to baked goods.

Brielle set up her table with shaking hands. Her candles sat in rows like little soldiers. Her logo was printed on a sign she had made on Canva. Bridget helped by handing out cards and smiling at strangers. By the end of the day, Brielle had sold 14 candles and passed out 30 business cards.

But the real win? A woman came up to her, picked up a candle, and said, "This smells like peace. I needed this today."

Brielle smiled, holding back tears. "I made it just for you."

That night, she wrote in her journal: *"I am the woman I used to pray to become."*

The Sisterhood That Carried Them

They didn't drift apart like most adult friendships do. They locked in. Every month, they met up, not to gossip or vent but to build. They'd bring notebooks, wine, dreams, and fears. The called it "CEO Circle," even when none of them were CEOs yet.

They'd text each other:

"Did you post your video today?"

"Make sure you charge you're worth."

"Take the nap, sis. Rest is productive."

They healed together. Failed together. Grew together.

HER Becomes Home

One summer evening, they met at a rooftop event downtown. Jasmine wore a flowing yellow dress, and her handmade keychains sold out in the first hour. Monique was the guest speaker on a panel for new content creators. Brielle's candles were in swag bags handed out to every guest. They clinked glasses, took selfies, and looked around at the life they were building.

"You realize we're HER now, right?" Jasmine said.

Monique laughed. "It's wild. And we did it with overdraft accounts, Target bras, and tears in the car."

Brielle whispered, "We did it scared. But we still did it."

And somewhere, deep inside each of them, a voice echoed: *"I was never lost. I was just buried. And now… I bloom."*

They Chose HER Too

Part 4:
The Becoming...
and the Big
Bang

This wasn't a glow-up. It was a burn up. Everything that wasn't true, wasn't healthy, wasn't aligned… had to be set on fire. And from the ashes? They emerged. Not perfect. Not polished. But finally HER. In her own way, on their own terms

The Identity Breakthrough

It happened differently for each of them…

Jasmine stood in front of her mirror one random Thursday night with her bonnet on, sweatpants sagging at the waist, cracked phone in one hand, and a chip bag in the other. She looked herself dead in the eyes and whispered:

"You're not lazy. You're tired of pretending to be everything. And from now on, you only carry what's yours to hold."

She dropped the guilt that night. Not all at once, but enough to start breathing again.

Monique finally spoke her truth out loud on her channel. She stared into the camera, makeup-free, voice trembling, and said:

"I almost gave up. Not just on content… but on myself. I almost settled. But God wouldn't let me rest. And if you're watching this, sis, neither should you. You deserve a life that feels like you."

That video got shared over 3,000 times. Not because it was flawless, but because it was honest.

Brielle turned down a promotion. Yep—the job she used to pray for? She said no. They offered her more money, more responsibility, and more hours. She thought about it. Prayed about it. Then said:

"Thank you, but no. I'm choosing peace over performance."

They looked at her like she was crazy. But she walked out of that meeting free.

The Ripple Effect

What started as a whisper inside them… started shaking everything around them. They made new friends. Attracted new opportunities. Set boundaries that made people uncomfortable. Began investing in themselves like they were allowed to win.

They stopped over-explaining. Stopped dimming their light. Stopped saying "maybe later" to dreams that were screaming *now.* Their kids saw it. Their partners felt it. Even their enemies couldn't deny it.

They weren't just surviving anymore. They were becoming.

The Breakdown That Becomes a Breakthrough

Let's be real. They had hard days. Still questioned everything. Still had moments when the fear came back louder than ever. But this time? They didn't fold. They faced it.

Because once you've seen yourself in your full power, in your full softness, in your full truth… you can't unsee it.

They weren't chasing HER anymore. They were HER. Even if their accounts were low. Even if the baby daddy was inconsistent. Even if they were healing from church hurt, daddy wounds, toxic friendships, or financial trauma.

They were still HER. Scarred but sacred. Bent but never broken. Healing is holy.

When HER Becomes a Movement

One Saturday, they hosted a women's brunch in the city. It started with 12 women in a small event space above a smoothie bar. No decor budget. No sponsors. No big brands. Just three woman, folding chairs, candles on the table, and stories that made the walls weep.

Jasmine shared how she overcame guilt.

Monique taught a mini content strategy session.

Brielle closed with a message titled:

"You Don't Need Permission to Begin Again."

Woman cried. They journaled. They hugged strangers like sisters. And when it was over, one young mom approached them with her baby on her hip and said:

"I didn't know women like y'all existed. I thought I had to figure this out alone. But now I see... I can become HER too." They smiled. Because they knew: the torched had been passed.

Final Reflection

Becoming HER is not a destination. It's a decision made every day, in every moment, especially when it's hardest. You don't wait until you're healed, rich, skinny, married, or confident. You choose HER now.

In the mess.

In the doubt.

In the struggle.

And then you keep choosing.

Group Affirmation from Brielle, Jasmine, & Monique... to YOU

I am no longer shrinking to survive. I am expanding to become.

I don't need all the answers to move forward. I just need to believe that I deserve more.

I am the breakthrough my bloodline prayed for. I am the first to go first.

I no longer carry guilt for putting myself first. I know that when I rise, everything connected to me rises too.

I walk in softness and strength.

I speak peace over pressure.

I hold space for both joy and healing.

I am choosing HER not someday, not when I "have it together," but right now.

The world will adjust to my becoming.

And if it doesn't?

That's okay. I didn't come to be understood. I came to be free.

I am HER.

Unmuted and Unbreakable.

About the Author

Triecia is a mother, a creator, a coach, and a woman who decided to stop surviving and finally start living.

Born and raised in the reality of responsibility, she knows what it feels like to be strong because there's no other choice. She spent years performing for approval, suppressing emotions, and trying to keep it all together… until she realized the version of herself she needed most was buried under everything she was told to be.

Now she is building a life rooted in peace, purpose, and personal freedom, and she's bringing as many women as she can with her.

As the founder of *The Becoming Her Journey* and *Serenity 920,* Triecia uses her platforms to help women, especially mothers, unmute their voices, break cycles, and reclaim the life they were always meant to live.

When she's not coaching, writing, or creating, she's dancing in the kitchen with her daughters, pouring candles in her workspace, or whispering affirmations to herself while pushing through hard days.

This book is not the end of her story. It is just the beginning of yours.

You can follow Triecia's journey, products, and coaching program:

- **Candle & Mindset Products:** *Serenity 920*

- **Coaching & Resources:** *TheBecomingHerJourney.com*

Personal Note From the Author

Dear sis,

You made it. Not just to the end of this book... but to the beginning of the rest of your life. If you feel a lump in your throat or a stirring in your spirit right now, that's confirmation. That's God saying,

"You are not too far gone. And this is not the end."

The journey we've taken together was more than words on a page. It was a mirror. It was meant to reflect the woman buried underneath the layers of trauma, expectations, silence, and survival.

I see you.

I was you.

And I'm walking this healing path with you.

I wrote this because I was once in a dark place emotionally, spiritually, and financially, wondering if the light would ever find me again. And when it did... I decided I wouldn't keep it to myself. Now, I want to help you take your own light and build a life you don't need a vacation from.

If your heart is tugging, if your mind is racing, if your soul is screaming, *"I want more. I just don't know where to start..."* that's where I come in.

I'm a life coach, but more than that, I'm proof.

Proof that you can heal.

Proof that you can build.

Proof that you can start over again and again and still win.

When you're ready, I'll be here to guide you, walk with you, and show you how to finally become HER, for real this time.

This isn't goodbye.

It's a sacred see you soon.

With love, power, and purpose,

Triecia

Coach. Creator. Chain Breaker.

Founder of *Her Purposeful Pursuit.*

This is your invitation to walk with me

If this book stirred something in you… if you saw pieces of yourself in every chapter and in every woman… if you're done pretending you're okay when you're not…

Then it's time.

Time to stop trying to figure it all out alone. Time to stop shrinking to fit into the version of you that everyone else is comfortable with. Time to stop waiting until you "have it all together" to take the first step.

You don't need to be perfect to begin.

You just have to be willing.

And if you're willing… I got you.

Introducing: The Becoming Her Journey

H.E.R.= Healed. Empowered. Reclaimed.

This isn't just a program... it's a process.

Together, we'll break the habits that are breaking you. We'll rewrite the narrative that's kept you quiet, small, and stuck. And we'll build a life that feels good to wake up to.

You'll get:

- Real strategies to break free from survival mode

- Support your healing emotionally, spiritually and mentally

- Tools to reclaim your time, identity, and peace

- Guidance to create your own version of freedom - financial, emotional, and spiritual

- A sisterhood of women who get it - and get you

You'll laugh. You'll cry. You'll grow.

But most of all... You'll rise.

You've spent enough time stuck.

Let's work together and finally break the cycle.

Join the waitlist or apply for coaching at:

thebecomingher.com

You became unmuted. You realized you're unbreakable.

Now it's time to become HER.